Scratch & Play
Peter Gordon

**PUZZLE
WRIGHT
PRESS**

An imprint of Sterling
Publishing Co., Inc.

www.puzzlewright.com

Puzzlewright Press and the distinctive Puzzlewright Press logo are registered trademarks of Sterling Publishing Co., Inc.

2   4   6   8   10   9   7   5   3

Published by Sterling Publishing Co., Inc.
387 Park Avenue South, New York, NY 10016
© 2007 Hasbro
Distributed in Canada by Sterling Publishing
C/o Canadian Manda Group, 165 Dufferin Street
Toronto, Ontario, Canada M6K 3H6
Distributed in the United Kingdom by GMC Distribution Services
Castle Place, 166 High Street, Lewes, East Sussex, England BN7 1XU
Distributed in Australia by Capricorn Link (Australia) Pty. Ltd.
P.O. Box 704, Windsor, NSW 2756, Australia

YAHTZEE is a trademark of Hasbro and is used with permission.
© 2007 Hasbro. All Rights Reserved.

Sterling ISBN 978-1-4027-5091-5

For information about custom editions, special sales, premium and
corporate purchases, please contact Sterling Special Sales
Department at 800-805-5489 or specialsales@sterlingpublishing.com.

Introduction

You are holding in your hands a revolution in gaming technology. No longer do you need a flat surface and five dice to play the classic game of YAHTZEE. A fingernail and a writing implement is all that's required to enjoy one of the finest games ever invented.

How to Play YAHTZEE

YAHTZEE is a simple-to-learn game whose object is to score as many points as possible in 13 turns. On each turn you roll five dice and then may reroll any or all of them one or two more times to create a final combination that is scored in one of the 13 scoring categories. Once a scoring category is filled, it can't be reused in that game, so deciding where to score a particular roll is part of the game's complex strategy. The scoresheet, found on page 9 and all the later odd-numbered pages, is divided into an Upper Section and a Lower Section. In the Upper Section, scores are determined by adding up the occurrences of the number whose category the roll is scored in. So, for example, a final roll of ⚃⚀⚃⚃⚄ would be worth 2 points in Twos, 9 points in Threes, 5 points in Fives, or 0 points in Aces, Fours, or Sixes. If your Upper Section total is worth 63 points or more, then you get a bonus of 35 points.

In the Lower Section, certain combinations must be achieved to score points in the categories. For 3 of a Kind, at least three of the dice must be the same. If so, you score the sum of the five dice. So ⚀⚀⚄⚀⚀ is worth 13 points, ⚁⚀⚂⚃⚄ is worth 21 points, and ⚀⚁⚂⚃⚄ is worth 0 points, since there's no 3 of a Kind. In 4 of a Kind, at least four dice must be the same, in which case you score the sum of the five dice. For example, ⚄⚄⚄⚂⚄ is worth 18 points, ⚁⚁⚁⚁⚄ is worth 24 points, and ⚀⚂⚃⚂⚀ is worth 0 points. The Full House category is worth 25 points if you have dice that can be divided into a pair and a three-of-a-kind. Thus, ⚂⚂⚀⚂⚀ and ⚀⚀⚀⚄⚄ would both score 25 points. Note that a hand with all five of the same dice can be scored for 25 points in Full House. To get a Small Straight, you need to have either ⚀⚁⚂⚃, ⚁⚂⚃⚄, or ⚂⚃⚄⚅ in some order among your five dice. If you do, you score 30 points. Here are some valid Small Straight hands: ⚂⚀⚃⚁⚄, ⚀⚁⚂⚃⚀, and ⚃⚄⚂⚀⚁. Large Straight is just like Small Straight, but longer and worth 40 points. The dice must be either ⚀⚁⚂⚃⚄ or ⚁⚂⚃⚄⚅ in any order. (A Large Straight can be scored in the Small Straight category for 30 points.) YAHTZEE is five dice of the same kind. It's worth 50 points. Two YAHTZEE examples: ⚁⚁⚁⚁⚁ and ⚅⚅⚅⚅⚅. Chance is the simplest category. You score the sum of the five dice. So ⚀⚁⚀⚄⚀ is worth 14 points, ⚀⚃⚄⚃⚁ is worth 19 points, and ⚁⚁⚃⚃⚃ is worth 20 points.

If you roll a YAHTZEE and you've already scored 50 points in your YAHTZEE category, you get a bonus of 100 points. Put a ✓ in the appropriate row, and at the end of the game, give yourself 100 points for each ✓ mark. If, however, you roll a YAHTZEE after scoring 0 in the YAHTZEE category, then you don't get the 100-point bonus. In either case, the roll must be scored in another category. But there is a special joker rule that applies when you roll a YAHTZEE. If the YAHTZEE category has a score in it (0 or 50), and the number in the Upper Section that matches your YAHTZEE also has been used, then you can use your roll as a joker. This means that the roll can be scored for 30 points in Small Straight or 40 points in Large Straight, in addition to the regular places you could normally score it (3 of a Kind, 4 of a Kind, Full House, and Chance). So, for example, if you roll ⚄⚄⚄⚄⚄ and you've already taken 0 in YAHTZEE and 15 in Fives, then if your Large Straight is available, you can score this roll as 40 in that category. (You'd get no YAHTZEE bonus of 100 points, though, since your YAHTZEE score was 0, not 50.)

How to Play YAHTZEE Scratch & Play

Here is a sample turn to see how the scratch-off aspect of the game works. You start by rubbing off the top row to reveal this:

You decide to keep the pair of 5's, so you scratch off the dice below the 2, 6, and 1, to reveal this:

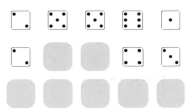

Now you have [dice], a Small Straight. You abandon your effort for 5's and instead go for a Large Straight by scratching off the silver in the third row under one of the 5's. Which one? This could be an important decision! Let's do the one under the first 5:

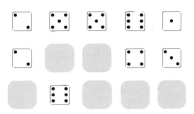

Yes! The final hand, consisting of the bottom die in each column, is [dice], a Large Straight. Nice job.

Competing Against the Book

After you have finished the game and totaled your score, you should then scratch off the oval next to "Peter's score" to see who won. No fair looking at that before you are done, since knowing what score you need to beat would be a huge advantage for you.

Below my score is the score achieved by the Optimal Solitaire YAHTZEE Player (OSYP). This program was developed by Tom Verhoeff of Technische Universiteit Eindhoven in the Netherlands (visit his Web site at http://www.win.tue.nl/~wstomv/misc/yahtzee/). OSYP assumes that the dice are truly random (which they are), and it aims to maximize the average final score over many games. It takes into account all future possibilities, and weighs them all according to their probabilities, and then chooses a move that results in the highest expected value. If two or more moves are optimal, it chooses the first encountered. Is it possible to beat OSYP? Yes. Sometimes playing optimally does not yield the highest score. For example, if the dice are laid out like the 15 below, and it's the last turn of a game in which all you need is a YAHTZEE, the proper strategy is to keep the four 5s and try to get a YAHTZEE in 5s. But with the dice as shown, that strategy will fail.

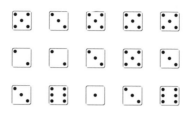

The only way to get a YAHTZEE with these dice is to keep just the 3 in the first turn, tossing away the four 5s. Then hold the 3s that you pick up on turn two and luck out with a pair of 3s on the final roll. If you do this regularly, you will have a terrible score, but in this case, it's the right move. OSYP always makes the move that will give it the best score over the long run, and in this case it would mean keeping the four 5s.

Another way to beat OSYP is if a situation arises where a random choice has to be made. If the dice show ⚃⚀⚄⚄⚅ and the proper strategy is to go for the Large Straight, then from a mathematical perspective it doesn't matter which ⚃ gets rerolled. But one ⚃ might have a ⚅ under it, while the other has a useless ⚀. If OSYP happens to pick the wrong ⚃, then you could eke out a victory. My record against it was 21 wins and 35 losses, with 4 ties. OSYP's average score was 247.1, while its theoretical average over an infinite number of games is 254.6. My average score was 234.0.

The maximum score is calculated by assuming you have x-ray vision, and can see all 195 dice at the start. It plays the game perfectly (so it would find the YAHTZEE in 3s in the example above), and you cannot beat its score. The average maximum score for the 60 games in this book is 337.8. The FreePascal program to generate these scores was also created by Tom Verhoeff, and I offer my sincere thanks for his efforts.

Two-Player Version

There are two ways to play YAHTZEE Scratch & Play with two players. The simplest is to pass the book back and forth between players and to play on two different pages. This is no different from a typical game with dice. But for a more interesting challenge, get two copies of the book. Then have both players turn to the same page, and play the game simultaneously. You can either announce your results after each turn or wait until the entire game is done. You'll have the exact same dice to choose from, so the element of luck will be largely eliminated.

—Peter Gordon

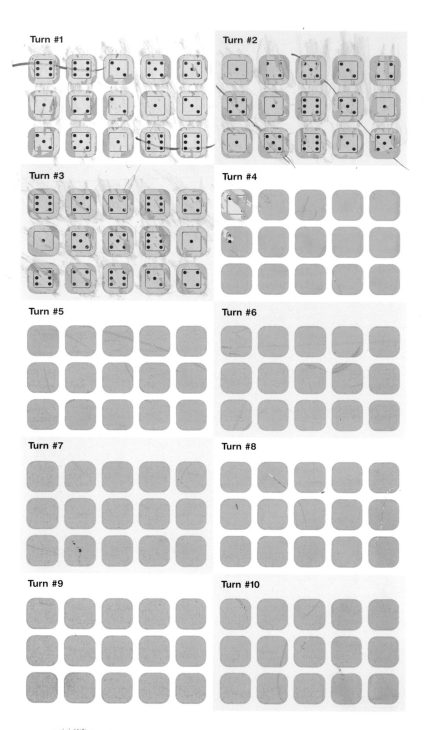

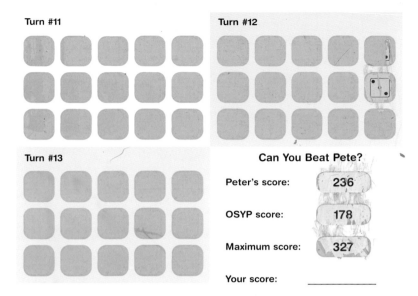

Turn #11

Turn #12

Turn #13

Can You Beat Pete?

Peter's score: 236

OSYP score: 178

Maximum score: 327

Your score: _____

Scratch & Play

UPPER SECTION		HOW TO SCORE	SCORE
Aces	· = 1	Count and Add Only Aces	
Twos	·· = 2	Count and Add Only Twos	
Threes	·.· = 3	Count and Add Only Threes	
Fours	:: = 4	Count and Add Only Fours	
Fives	:·: = 5	Count and Add Only Fives	
Sixes	::: = 6	Count and Add Only Sixes	2 4
TOTAL SCORE		⟶	
BONUS	If total score is 63 or over	SCORE 35	
TOTAL	Of Upper Section	⟶	
LOWER SECTION			
3 of a Kind		Add Total of All Dice	
4 of a Kind		Add Total of All Dice	
Full House		SCORE 25	
Sm. Straight	Sequence of 4	SCORE 30	
Lg. Straight	Sequence of 5	SCORE 40	
YAHTZEE	5 of a kind	SCORE 50	✓
Chance		Add Total of All 5 Dice	
YAHTZEE BONUS		✓ FOR EACH BONUS	
		SCORE 100 PER ✓	
TOTAL	Of Lower Section	⟶	
TOTAL	Of Upper Section	⟶	
GRAND TOTAL		⟶	

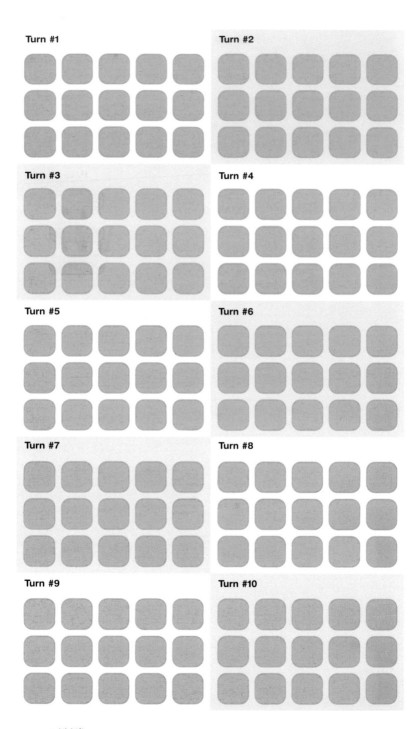

Turn #1

Turn #2

Turn #3

Turn #4

Turn #5

Turn #6

Turn #7

Turn #8

Turn #9

Turn #10

Turn #11

Turn #12

Turn #13

Can You Beat Pete?

Peter's score:

OSYP score:

Maximum score:

Your score: _____

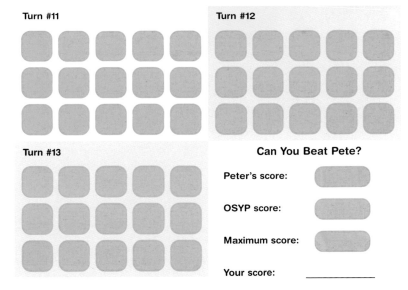

Yahtzee Scratch & Play

UPPER SECTION		HOW TO SCORE	SCORE
Aces	⊡ = 1	Count and Add Only Aces	
Twos	⊡ = 2	Count and Add Only Twos	
Threes	⊡ = 3	Count and Add Only Threes	
Fours	⊡ = 4	Count and Add Only Fours	
Fives	⊡ = 5	Count and Add Only Fives	
Sixes	⊡ = 6	Count and Add Only Sixes	
TOTAL SCORE		⟶	
BONUS	If total score is 63 or over	SCORE 35	
TOTAL	Of Upper Section	⟶	
LOWER SECTION			
3 of a Kind		Add Total of All Dice	
4 of a Kind		Add Total of All Dice	
Full House		SCORE 25	
Sm. Straight	Sequence of 4	SCORE 30	
Lg. Straight	Sequence of 5	SCORE 40	
YAHTZEE	5 of a kind	SCORE 50	
Chance		Add Total of All 5 Dice	
YAHTZEE BONUS		✓ FOR EACH BONUS	
		SCORE 100 PER ✓	
TOTAL	Of Lower Section	⟶	
TOTAL	Of Upper Section	⟶	
GRAND TOTAL		⟶	

Turn #1

Turn #2

Turn #3

Turn #4

Turn #5

Turn #6

Turn #7

Turn #8

Turn #9

Turn #10

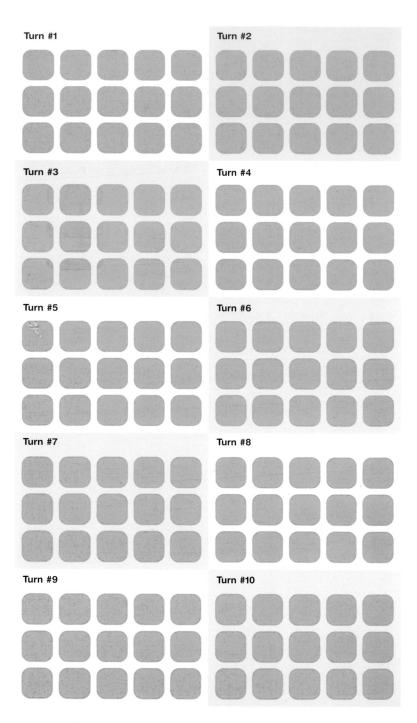

Turn #11

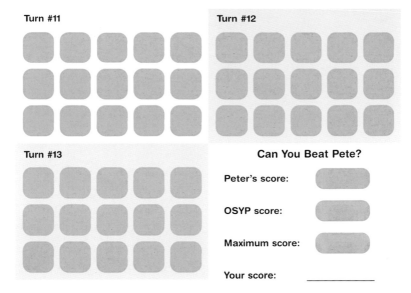

Turn #12

Turn #13

Can You Beat Pete?

Peter's score:

OSYP score:

Maximum score:

Your score: _____

Scratch & Play

UPPER SECTION		HOW TO SCORE	SCORE
Aces	⚀ = 1	Count and Add Only Aces	
Twos	⚁ = 2	Count and Add Only Twos	
Threes	⚂ = 3	Count and Add Only Threes	
Fours	⚃ = 4	Count and Add Only Fours	
Fives	⚄ = 5	Count and Add Only Fives	
Sixes	⚅ = 6	Count and Add Only Sixes	
TOTAL SCORE		⟶	
BONUS	If total score is 63 or over	SCORE 35	
TOTAL	Of Upper Section	⟶	
LOWER SECTION			
3 of a Kind		Add Total of All Dice	
4 of a Kind		Add Total of All Dice	
Full House		SCORE 25	
Sm. Straight	Sequence of 4	SCORE 30	
Lg. Straight	Sequence of 5	SCORE 40	
YAHTZEE	5 of a kind	SCORE 50	
Chance		Add Total of All 5 Dice	
YAHTZEE BONUS		✓ FOR EACH BONUS	
		SCORE 100 PER ✓	
TOTAL	Of Lower Section	⟶	
TOTAL	Of Upper Section	⟶	
GRAND TOTAL		⟶	

Turn #1

Turn #2

Turn #3

Turn #4

Turn #5

Turn #6

Turn #7

Turn #8

Turn #9

Turn #10

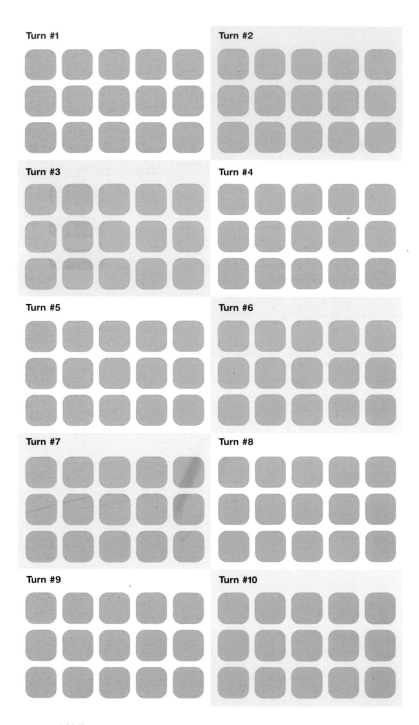

Turn #11

Turn #12

Turn #13

Can You Beat Pete?

Peter's score:

OSYP score:

Maximum score:

Your score: _____

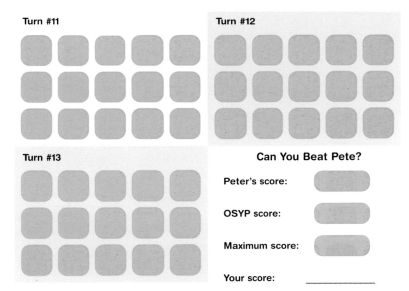

Scratch & Play

UPPER SECTION		HOW TO SCORE	SCORE
Aces	⚀ = 1	Count and Add Only Aces	
Twos	⚁ = 2	Count and Add Only Twos	
Threes	⚂ = 3	Count and Add Only Threes	
Fours	⚃ = 4	Count and Add Only Fours	
Fives	⚄ = 5	Count and Add Only Fives	
Sixes	⚅ = 6	Count and Add Only Sixes	
TOTAL SCORE		➡	
BONUS	If total score is 63 or over	SCORE 35	
TOTAL	Of Upper Section	➡	
LOWER SECTION			
3 of a Kind		Add Total of All Dice	
4 of a Kind		Add Total of All Dice	
Full House		SCORE 25	
Sm. Straight	Sequence of 4	SCORE 30	
Lg. Straight	Sequence of 5	SCORE 40	
YAHTZEE	5 of a kind	SCORE 50	
Chance		Add Total of All 5 Dice	
YAHTZEE BONUS		✓ FOR EACH BONUS	
		SCORE 100 PER ✓	
TOTAL	Of Lower Section	➡	
TOTAL	Of Upper Section	➡	
GRAND TOTAL		➡	

Turn #1

Turn #2

Turn #3

Turn #4

Turn #5

Turn #6

Turn #7

Turn #8

Turn #9

Turn #10

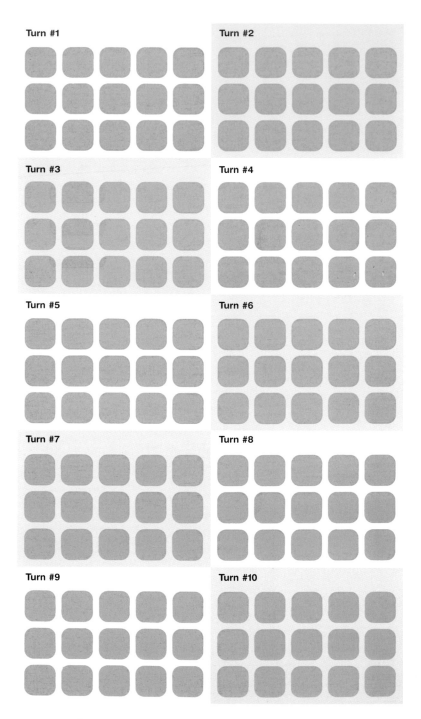

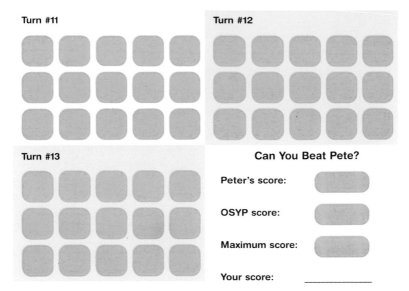

Turn #11

Turn #12

Turn #13

Can You Beat Pete?

Peter's score:

OSYP score:

Maximum score:

Your score: _____

Scratch & Play

UPPER SECTION		HOW TO SCORE	SCORE
Aces	$\boxdot$ = 1	Count and Add Only Aces	
Twos	$\boxdot$ = 2	Count and Add Only Twos	
Threes	$\boxdot$ = 3	Count and Add Only Threes	
Fours	$\boxdot$ = 4	Count and Add Only Fours	
Fives	$\boxdot$ = 5	Count and Add Only Fives	
Sixes	$\boxdot$ = 6	Count and Add Only Sixes	
TOTAL SCORE		⟶	
BONUS	If total score is 63 or over	SCORE 35	
TOTAL	Of Upper Section	⟶	
LOWER SECTION			
3 of a Kind		Add Total of All Dice	
4 of a Kind		Add Total of All Dice	
Full House		SCORE 25	
Sm. Straight	Sequence of 4	SCORE 30	
Lg. Straight	Sequence of 5	SCORE 40	
YAHTZEE	5 of a kind	SCORE 50	
Chance		Add Total of All 5 Dice	
YAHTZEE BONUS		✓ FOR EACH BONUS	
		SCORE 100 PER ✓	
TOTAL	Of Lower Section	⟶	
TOTAL	Of Upper Section	⟶	
GRAND TOTAL		⟶	

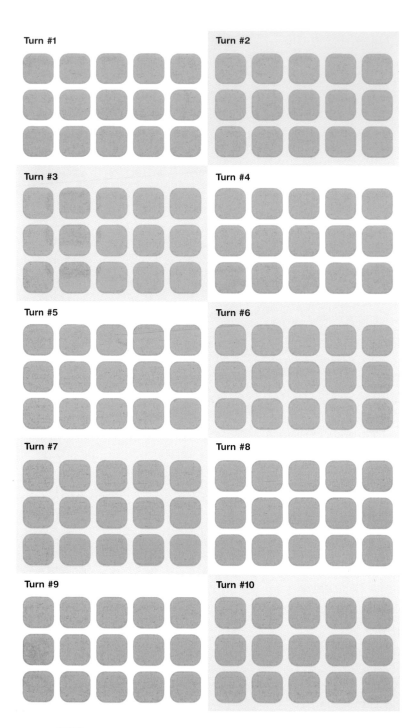

Turn #11

Turn #12

Turn #13

Can You Beat Pete?

Peter's score:

OSYP score:

Maximum score:

Your score: _____

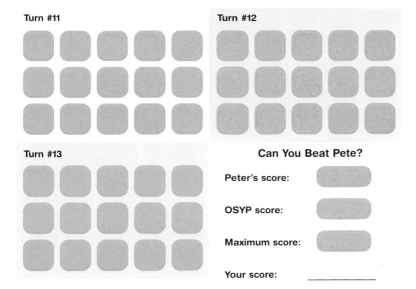

Scratch & Play

UPPER SECTION		HOW TO SCORE	SCORE
Aces	• = 1	Count and Add Only Aces	
Twos	▫ = 2	Count and Add Only Twos	
Threes	∴ = 3	Count and Add Only Threes	
Fours	∷ = 4	Count and Add Only Fours	
Fives	∷ = 5	Count and Add Only Fives	
Sixes	∷ = 6	Count and Add Only Sixes	
TOTAL SCORE		⟶	
BONUS	If total score is 63 or over	SCORE 35	
TOTAL	Of Upper Section	⟶	
LOWER SECTION			
3 of a Kind		Add Total of All Dice	
4 of a Kind		Add Total of All Dice	
Full House		SCORE 25	
Sm. Straight	Sequence of 4	SCORE 30	
Lg. Straight	Sequence of 5	SCORE 40	
YAHTZEE	5 of a kind	SCORE 50	
Chance		Add Total of All 5 Dice	
YAHTZEE BONUS		✓ FOR EACH BONUS	
		SCORE 100 PER ✓	
TOTAL	Of Lower Section	⟶	
TOTAL	Of Upper Section	⟶	
GRAND TOTAL		⟶	

Turn #1

Turn #2

Turn #3

Turn #4

Turn #5

Turn #6

Turn #7

Turn #8

Turn #9

Turn #10

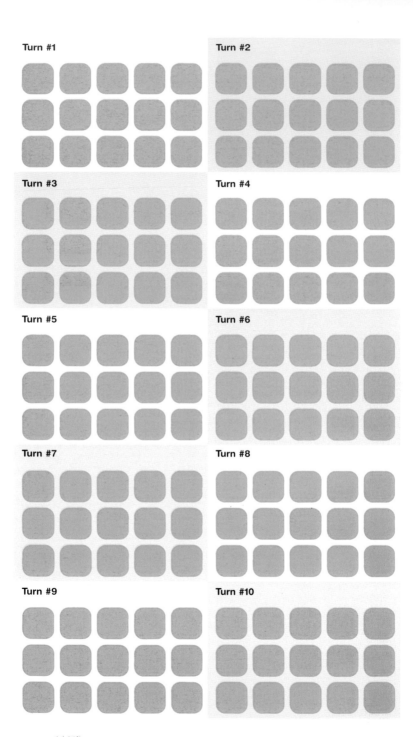

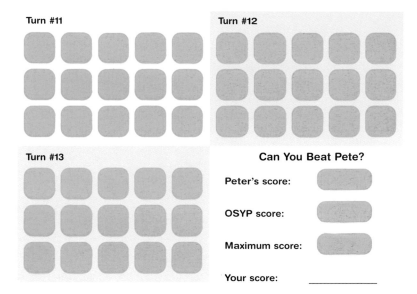

Turn #11

Turn #12

Turn #13

Can You Beat Pete?

Peter's score:

OSYP score:

Maximum score:

Your score: _____

Yahtzee Scratch & Play

UPPER SECTION		HOW TO SCORE	SCORE
Aces	⚀ = 1	Count and Add Only Aces	
Twos	⚁ = 2	Count and Add Only Twos	
Threes	⚂ = 3	Count and Add Only Threes	
Fours	⚃ = 4	Count and Add Only Fours	
Fives	⚄ = 5	Count and Add Only Fives	
Sixes	⚅ = 6	Count and Add Only Sixes	
TOTAL SCORE		⟶	
BONUS	If total score is 63 or over	SCORE 35	
TOTAL	Of Upper Section	⟶	
LOWER SECTION			
3 of a Kind		Add Total of All Dice	
4 of a Kind		Add Total of All Dice	
Full House		SCORE 25	
Sm. Straight	Sequence of 4	SCORE 30	
Lg. Straight	Sequence of 5	SCORE 40	
YAHTZEE	5 of a kind	SCORE 50	
Chance		Add Total of All 5 Dice	
YAHTZEE BONUS		✓ FOR EACH BONUS	
		SCORE 100 PER ✓	
TOTAL	Of Lower Section	⟶	
TOTAL	Of Upper Section	⟶	
GRAND TOTAL		⟶	

Turn #1

Turn #2

Turn #3

Turn #4

Turn #5

Turn #6

Turn #7

Turn #8

Turn #9

Turn #10

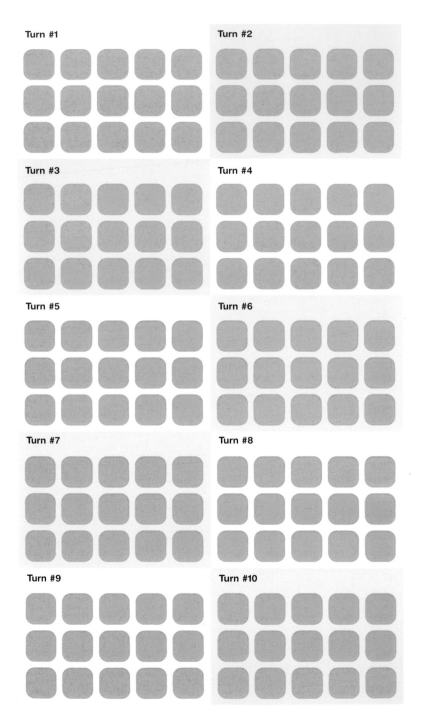

Turn #11

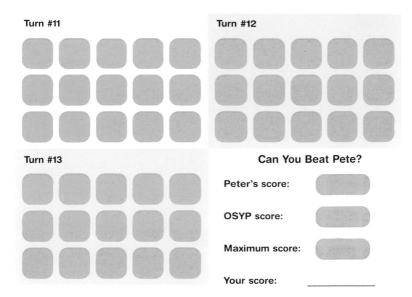

Turn #12

Turn #13

Can You Beat Pete?

Peter's score:

OSYP score:

Maximum score:

Your score: _____

Yahtzee Scratch & Play

UPPER SECTION		HOW TO SCORE	SCORE
Aces	�× = 1	Count and Add Only Aces	
Twos	⚁ = 2	Count and Add Only Twos	
Threes	⚂ = 3	Count and Add Only Threes	
Fours	⚃ = 4	Count and Add Only Fours	
Fives	⚄ = 5	Count and Add Only Fives	
Sixes	⚅ = 6	Count and Add Only Sixes	
TOTAL SCORE		⟶	
BONUS	If total score is 63 or over	SCORE 35	
TOTAL	Of Upper Section	⟶	
LOWER SECTION			
3 of a Kind		Add Total of All Dice	
4 of a Kind		Add Total of All Dice	
Full House		SCORE 25	
Sm. Straight	Sequence of 4	SCORE 30	
Lg. Straight	Sequence of 5	SCORE 40	
YAHTZEE	5 of a kind	SCORE 50	
Chance		Add Total of All 5 Dice	
YAHTZEE BONUS		✓ FOR EACH BONUS	
		SCORE 100 PER ✓	
TOTAL	Of Lower Section	⟶	
TOTAL	Of Upper Section	⟶	
GRAND TOTAL		⟶	

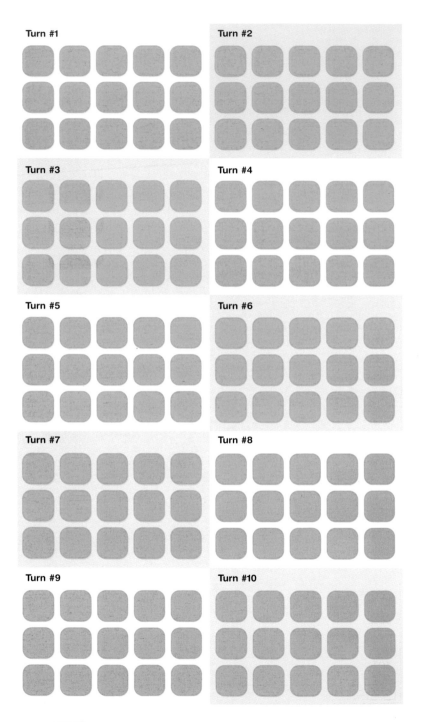

Turn #1

Turn #2

Turn #3

Turn #4

Turn #5

Turn #6

Turn #7

Turn #8

Turn #9

Turn #10

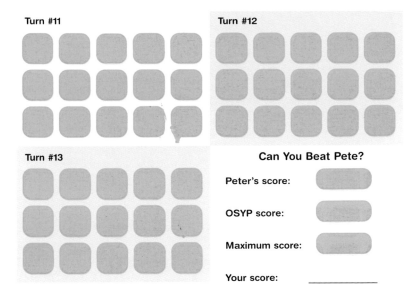

Turn #11

Turn #12

Turn #13

Can You Beat Pete?

Peter's score:

OSYP score:

Maximum score:

Your score: _____

Yahtzee Scratch & Play

UPPER SECTION		HOW TO SCORE	SCORE
Aces	⚀ = 1	Count and Add Only Aces	
Twos	⚁ = 2	Count and Add Only Twos	
Threes	⚂ = 3	Count and Add Only Threes	
Fours	⚃ = 4	Count and Add Only Fours	
Fives	⚄ = 5	Count and Add Only Fives	
Sixes	⚅ = 6	Count and Add Only Sixes	
TOTAL SCORE		⟶	
BONUS	If total score is 63 or over	SCORE 35	
TOTAL	Of Upper Section	⟶	
LOWER SECTION			
3 of a Kind		Add Total of All Dice	
4 of a Kind		Add Total of All Dice	
Full House		SCORE 25	
Sm. Straight	Sequence of 4	SCORE 30	
Lg. Straight	Sequence of 5	SCORE 40	
YAHTZEE	5 of a kind	SCORE 50	
Chance		Add Total of All 5 Dice	
YAHTZEE BONUS		✓ FOR EACH BONUS	
		SCORE 100 PER ✓	
TOTAL	Of Lower Section	⟶	
TOTAL	Of Upper Section	⟶	
GRAND TOTAL		⟶	

Turn #1

Turn #2

Turn #3

Turn #4

Turn #5

Turn #6

Turn #7

Turn #8

Turn #9

Turn #10

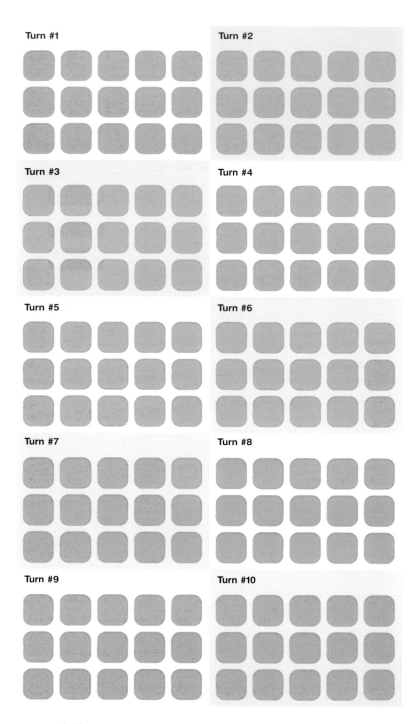

Turn #11

Turn #12

Turn #13

Can You Beat Pete?

Peter's score:

OSYP score:

Maximum score:

Your score: _____

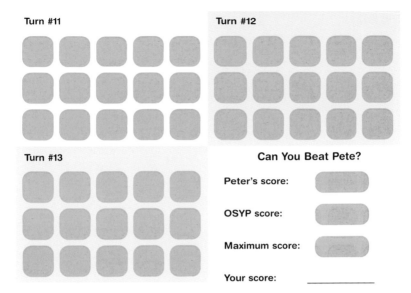

Yahtzee Scratch & Play

UPPER SECTION		HOW TO SCORE	SCORE
Aces	· = 1	Count and Add Only Aces	
Twos	·· = 2	Count and Add Only Twos	
Threes	··· = 3	Count and Add Only Threes	
Fours	···· = 4	Count and Add Only Fours	
Fives	····· = 5	Count and Add Only Fives	
Sixes	······ = 6	Count and Add Only Sixes	
TOTAL SCORE		⟶	
BONUS	If total score is 63 or over	SCORE 35	
TOTAL	Of Upper Section	⟶	
LOWER SECTION			
3 of a Kind		Add Total of All Dice	
4 of a Kind		Add Total of All Dice	
Full House		SCORE 25	
Sm. Straight	Sequence of 4	SCORE 30	
Lg. Straight	Sequence of 5	SCORE 40	
YAHTZEE	5 of a kind	SCORE 50	
Chance		Add Total of All 5 Dice	
YAHTZEE BONUS		✓ FOR EACH BONUS	
		SCORE 100 PER ✓	
TOTAL	Of Lower Section	⟶	
TOTAL	Of Upper Section	⟶	
GRAND TOTAL		⟶	

Turn #1

Turn #2

Turn #3

Turn #4

Turn #5

Turn #6

Turn #7

Turn #8

Turn #9

Turn #10

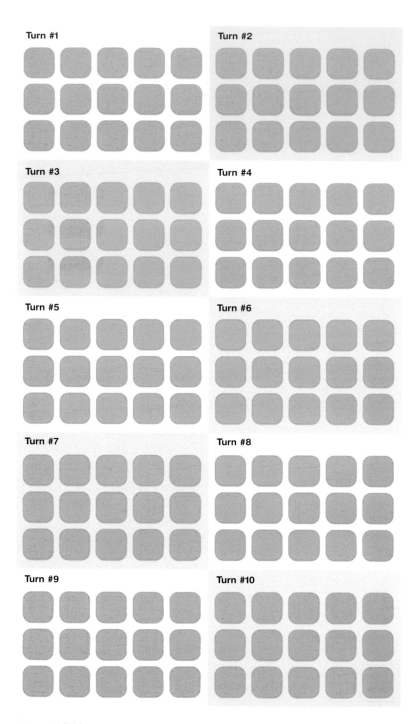

Turn #11

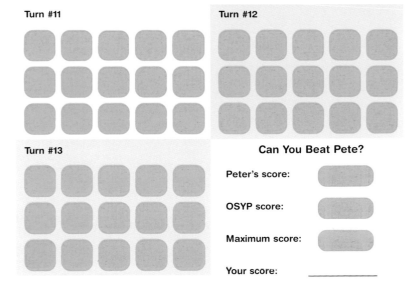

Turn #12

Turn #13

Can You Beat Pete?

Peter's score:

OSYP score:

Maximum score:

Your score: _____

~~Yahtzee~~ Scratch & Play

UPPER SECTION		HOW TO SCORE	SCORE
Aces	⚀ = 1	Count and Add Only Aces	
Twos	⚁ = 2	Count and Add Only Twos	
Threes	⚂ = 3	Count and Add Only Threes	
Fours	⚃ = 4	Count and Add Only Fours	
Fives	⚄ = 5	Count and Add Only Fives	
Sixes	⚅ = 6	Count and Add Only Sixes	
TOTAL SCORE		⟶	
BONUS	If total score is 63 or over	SCORE 35	
TOTAL	Of Upper Section	⟶	
LOWER SECTION			
3 of a Kind		Add Total of All Dice	
4 of a Kind		Add Total of All Dice	
Full House		SCORE 25	
Sm. Straight	Sequence of 4	SCORE 30	
Lg. Straight	Sequence of 5	SCORE 40	
YAHTZEE	5 of a kind	SCORE 50	
Chance		Add Total of All 5 Dice	
YAHTZEE BONUS		✓ FOR EACH BONUS	
		SCORE 100 PER ✓	
TOTAL	Of Lower Section	⟶	
TOTAL	Of Upper Section	⟶	
GRAND TOTAL		⟶	

Turn #1

Turn #2

Turn #3

Turn #4

Turn #5

Turn #6

Turn #7

Turn #8

Turn #9

Turn #10

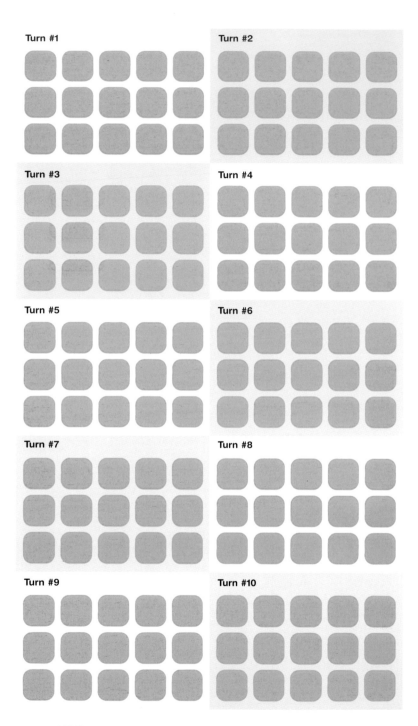

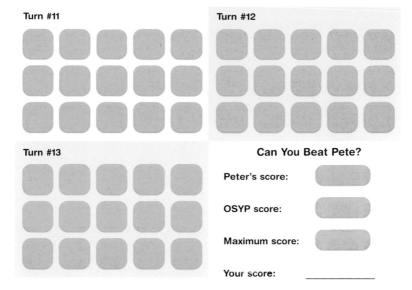

Turn #11

Turn #12

Turn #13

Can You Beat Pete?

Peter's score:

OSYP score:

Maximum score:

Your score: _____

~~Yahtzee~~ **Scratch & Play**

UPPER SECTION		HOW TO SCORE	SCORE
Aces	· = 1	Count and Add Only Aces	
Twos	·· = 2	Count and Add Only Twos	
Threes	·.· = 3	Count and Add Only Threes	
Fours	:: = 4	Count and Add Only Fours	
Fives	:·: = 5	Count and Add Only Fives	
Sixes	::: = 6	Count and Add Only Sixes	
TOTAL SCORE		⟶	
BONUS	If total score is 63 or over	SCORE 35	
TOTAL	Of Upper Section	⟶	
LOWER SECTION			
3 of a Kind		Add Total of All Dice	
4 of a Kind		Add Total of All Dice	
Full House		SCORE 25	
Sm. Straight	Sequence of 4	SCORE 30	
Lg. Straight	Sequence of 5	SCORE 40	
YAHTZEE	5 of a kind	SCORE 50	
Chance		Add Total of All 5 Dice	
YAHTZEE BONUS		✓ FOR EACH BONUS	
		SCORE 100 PER ✓	
TOTAL	Of Lower Section	⟶	
TOTAL	Of Upper Section	⟶	
GRAND TOTAL		⟶	

Turn #1

Turn #2

Turn #3

Turn #4

Turn #5

Turn #6

Turn #7

Turn #8

Turn #9

Turn #10

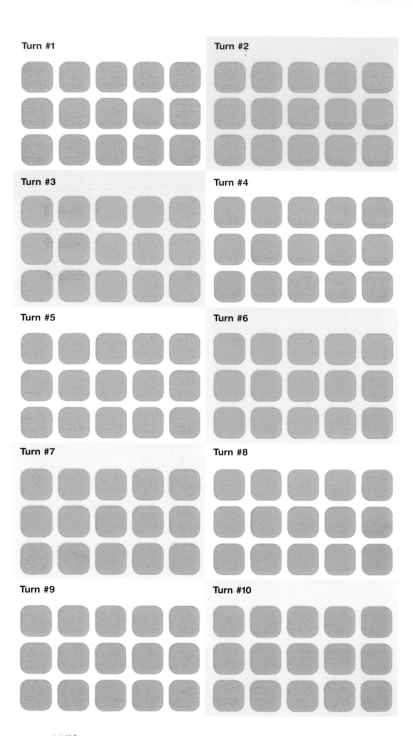

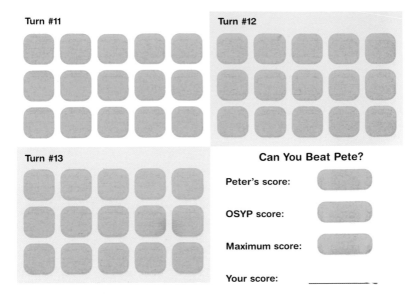

Turn #11

Turn #12

Turn #13

Can You Beat Pete?

Peter's score:

OSYP score:

Maximum score:

Your score: _____

Yahtzee Scratch & Play

UPPER SECTION		HOW TO SCORE	SCORE
Aces	⚀ = 1	Count and Add Only Aces	
Twos	⚁ = 2	Count and Add Only Twos	
Threes	⚂ = 3	Count and Add Only Threes	
Fours	⚃ = 4	Count and Add Only Fours	
Fives	⚄ = 5	Count and Add Only Fives	
Sixes	⚅ = 6	Count and Add Only Sixes	
TOTAL SCORE		⟶	
BONUS	If total score is 63 or over	SCORE 35	
TOTAL	Of Upper Section	⟶	
LOWER SECTION			
3 of a Kind		Add Total of All Dice	
4 of a Kind		Add Total of All Dice	
Full House		SCORE 25	
Sm. Straight	Sequence of 4	SCORE 30	
Lg. Straight	Sequence of 5	SCORE 40	
YAHTZEE	5 of a kind	SCORE 50	
Chance		Add Total of All 5 Dice	
YAHTZEE BONUS		✓ FOR EACH BONUS	
		SCORE 100 PER ✓	
TOTAL	Of Lower Section	⟶	
TOTAL	Of Upper Section	⟶	
GRAND TOTAL		⟶	

Turn #1

Turn #2

Turn #3

Turn #4

Turn #5

Turn #6

Turn #7

Turn #8

Turn #9

Turn #10

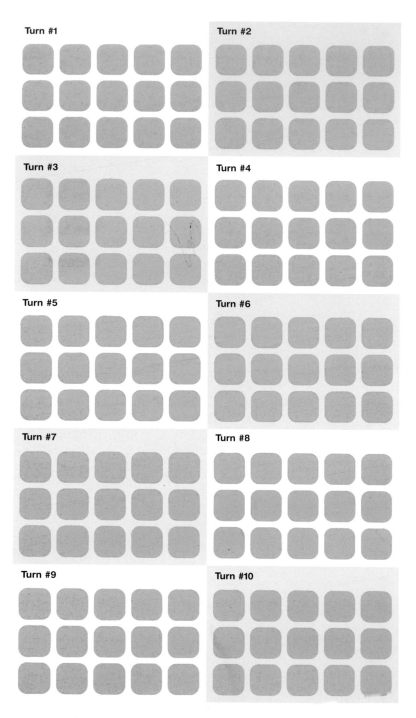

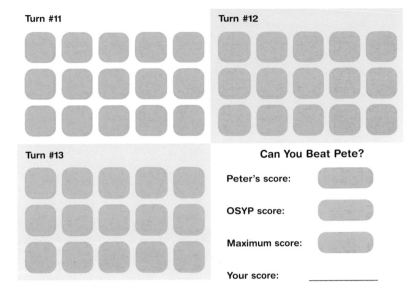

Turn #11

Turn #12

Turn #13

Can You Beat Pete?

Peter's score:

OSYP score:

Maximum score:

Your score: _____

Yahtzee Scratch & Play

UPPER SECTION		HOW TO SCORE	SCORE
Aces	⋅ = 1	Count and Add Only Aces	
Twos	= 2	Count and Add Only Twos	
Threes	= 3	Count and Add Only Threes	
Fours	= 4	Count and Add Only Fours	
Fives	= 5	Count and Add Only Fives	
Sixes	= 6	Count and Add Only Sixes	
TOTAL SCORE		⟶	
BONUS	If total score is 63 or over	SCORE 35	
TOTAL	Of Upper Section	⟶	
LOWER SECTION			
3 of a Kind		Add Total of All Dice	
4 of a Kind		Add Total of All Dice	
Full House		SCORE 25	
Sm. Straight	Sequence of 4	SCORE 30	
Lg. Straight	Sequence of 5	SCORE 40	
YAHTZEE	5 of a kind	SCORE 50	
Chance		Add Total of All 5 Dice	
YAHTZEE BONUS		✓ FOR EACH BONUS	
		SCORE 100 PER ✓	
TOTAL	Of Lower Section	⟶	
TOTAL	Of Upper Section	⟶	
GRAND TOTAL		⟶	

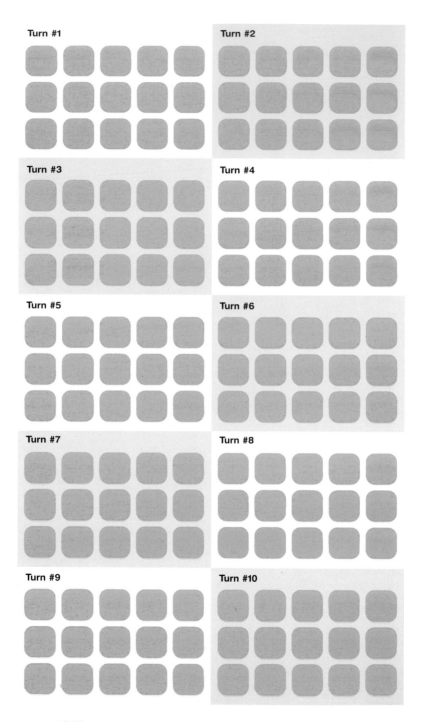

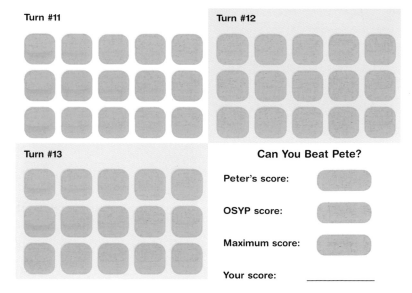

Turn #11

Turn #12

Turn #13

Can You Beat Pete?

Peter's score:

OSYP score:

Maximum score:

Your score: _____

Yahtzee Scratch & Play

UPPER SECTION		HOW TO SCORE	SCORE
Aces	• = 1	Count and Add Only Aces	
Twos	⦂ = 2	Count and Add Only Twos	
Threes	⦂ = 3	Count and Add Only Threes	
Fours	⦂ = 4	Count and Add Only Fours	
Fives	⦂ = 5	Count and Add Only Fives	
Sixes	⦂ = 6	Count and Add Only Sixes	
TOTAL SCORE		⟶	
BONUS	If total score is 63 or over	SCORE 35	
TOTAL	Of Upper Section	⟶	
LOWER SECTION			
3 of a Kind		Add Total of All Dice	
4 of a Kind		Add Total of All Dice	
Full House		SCORE 25	
Sm. Straight	Sequence of 4	SCORE 30	
Lg. Straight	Sequence of 5	SCORE 40	
YAHTZEE	5 of a kind	SCORE 50	
Chance		Add Total of All 5 Dice	
YAHTZEE BONUS		✓ FOR EACH BONUS	
		SCORE 100 PER ✓	
TOTAL	Of Lower Section	⟶	
TOTAL	Of Upper Section	⟶	
GRAND TOTAL		⟶	

Turn #1

Turn #2

Turn #3

Turn #4

Turn #5

Turn #6

Turn #7

Turn #8

Turn #9

Turn #10

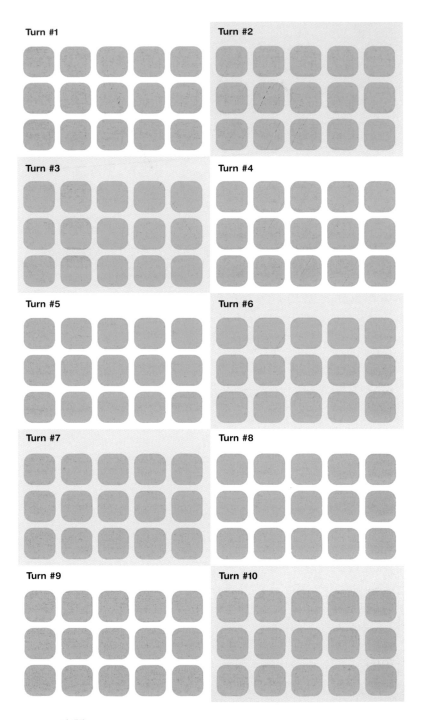

Turn #11

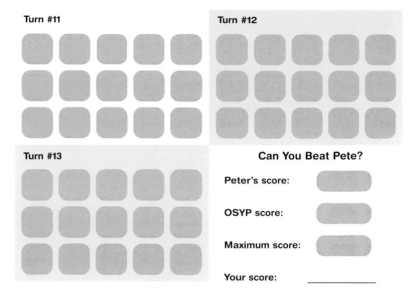

Turn #12

Turn #13

Can You Beat Pete?

Peter's score:

OSYP score:

Maximum score:

Your score: _____

Scratch & Play

UPPER SECTION		HOW TO SCORE	SCORE
Aces	⊡ = 1	Count and Add Only Aces	
Twos	⊡ = 2	Count and Add Only Twos	
Threes	⊡ = 3	Count and Add Only Threes	
Fours	⊡ = 4	Count and Add Only Fours	
Fives	⊡ = 5	Count and Add Only Fives	
Sixes	⊡ = 6	Count and Add Only Sixes	
TOTAL SCORE		⟶	
BONUS	If total score is 63 or over	SCORE 35	
TOTAL	Of Upper Section	⟶	
LOWER SECTION			
3 of a Kind		Add Total of All Dice	
4 of a Kind		Add Total of All Dice	
Full House		SCORE 25	
Sm. Straight	Sequence of 4	SCORE 30	
Lg. Straight	Sequence of 5	SCORE 40	
YAHTZEE	5 of a kind	SCORE 50	
Chance		Add Total of All 5 Dice	
YAHTZEE BONUS		✓ FOR EACH BONUS	
		SCORE 100 PER ✓	
TOTAL	Of Lower Section	⟶	
TOTAL	Of Upper Section	⟶	
GRAND TOTAL		⟶	

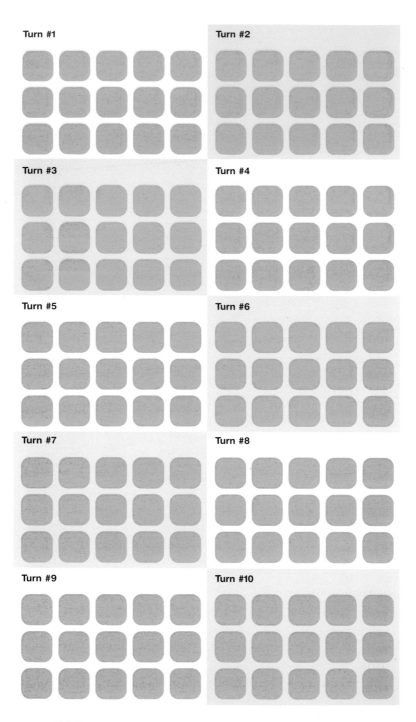

Turn #1

Turn #2

Turn #3

Turn #4

Turn #5

Turn #6

Turn #7

Turn #8

Turn #9

Turn #10

Turn #11

Turn #12

Turn #13

Can You Beat Pete?

Peter's score:

OSYP score:

Maximum score:

Your score: _____

Yahtzee Scratch & Play

UPPER SECTION		HOW TO SCORE	SCORE
Aces	⢀ = 1	Count and Add Only Aces	
Twos	⣀ = 2	Count and Add Only Twos	
Threes	⠢ = 3	Count and Add Only Threes	
Fours	⣒ = 4	Count and Add Only Fours	
Fives	⣢ = 5	Count and Add Only Fives	
Sixes	⣶ = 6	Count and Add Only Sixes	
TOTAL SCORE		⟶	
BONUS	If total score is 63 or over	SCORE 35	
TOTAL	Of Upper Section	⟶	
LOWER SECTION			
3 of a Kind		Add Total of All Dice	
4 of a Kind		Add Total of All Dice	
Full House		SCORE 25	
Sm. Straight	Sequence of 4	SCORE 30	
Lg. Straight	Sequence of 5	SCORE 40	
YAHTZEE	5 of a kind	SCORE 50	
Chance		Add Total of All 5 Dice	
YAHTZEE BONUS		✓ FOR EACH BONUS	
		SCORE 100 PER ✓	
TOTAL	Of Lower Section	⟶	
TOTAL	Of Upper Section	⟶	
GRAND TOTAL		⟶	

Turn #1

Turn #2

Turn #3

Turn #4

Turn #5

Turn #6

Turn #7

Turn #8

Turn #9

Turn #10

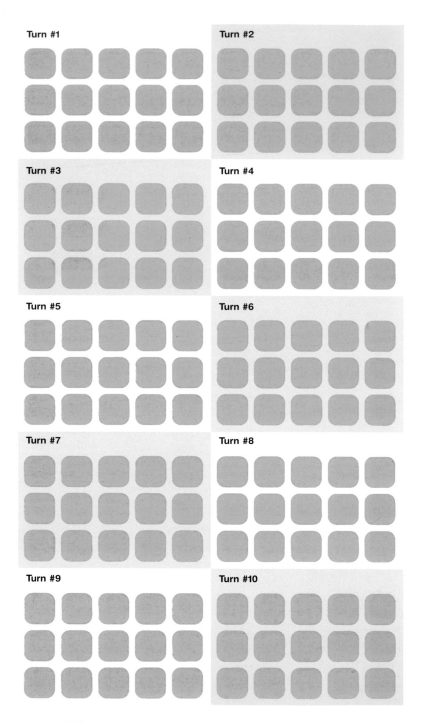

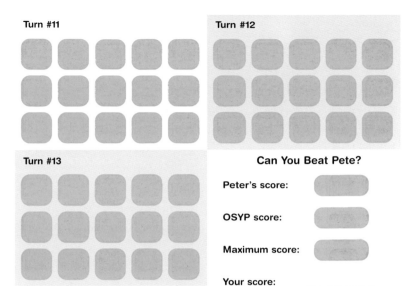

Turn #11

Turn #12

Turn #13

Can You Beat Pete?

Peter's score:

OSYP score:

Maximum score:

Your score: _____

Y̶a̶h̶t̶z̶e̶e̶ Scratch & Play

UPPER SECTION		HOW TO SCORE	SCORE
Aces	⚀ = 1	Count and Add Only Aces	
Twos	⚁ = 2	Count and Add Only Twos	
Threes	⚂ = 3	Count and Add Only Threes	
Fours	⚃ = 4	Count and Add Only Fours	
Fives	⚄ = 5	Count and Add Only Fives	
Sixes	⚅ = 6	Count and Add Only Sixes	
TOTAL SCORE		⟶	
BONUS	If total score is 63 or over	SCORE 35	
TOTAL	Of Upper Section	⟶	
LOWER SECTION			
3 of a Kind		Add Total of All Dice	
4 of a Kind		Add Total of All Dice	
Full House		SCORE 25	
Sm. Straight	Sequence of 4	SCORE 30	
Lg. Straight	Sequence of 5	SCORE 40	
YAHTZEE	5 of a kind	SCORE 50	
Chance		Add Total of All 5 Dice	
YAHTZEE BONUS		✓ FOR EACH BONUS	
		SCORE 100 PER ✓	
TOTAL	Of Lower Section	⟶	
TOTAL	Of Upper Section	⟶	
GRAND TOTAL		⟶	

Turn #1

Turn #2

Turn #3

Turn #4

Turn #5

Turn #6

Turn #7

Turn #8

Turn #9

Turn #10

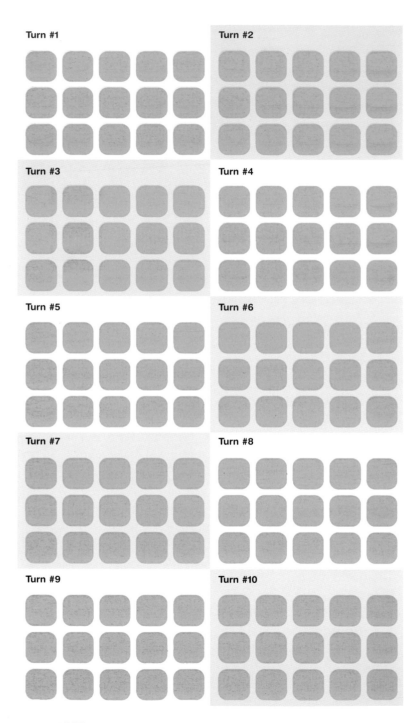

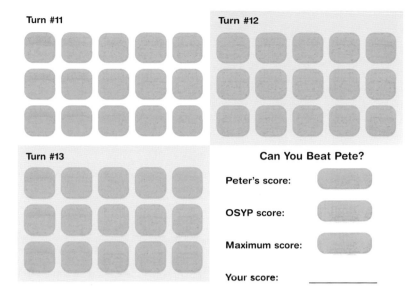

Turn #11

Turn #12

Turn #13

Can You Beat Pete?

Peter's score:

OSYP score:

Maximum score:

Your score: _____

Yahtzee Scratch & Play

UPPER SECTION		HOW TO SCORE	SCORE
Aces	$\cdot$ = 1	Count and Add Only Aces	
Twos	$\vdots$ = 2	Count and Add Only Twos	
Threes	$\therefore$ = 3	Count and Add Only Threes	
Fours	$\vdots\vdots$ = 4	Count and Add Only Fours	
Fives	$\because$ = 5	Count and Add Only Fives	
Sixes	$\vdots\vdots$ = 6	Count and Add Only Sixes	
TOTAL SCORE		⟶	
BONUS	If total score is 63 or over	SCORE 35	
TOTAL	Of Upper Section	⟶	
LOWER SECTION			
3 of a Kind		Add Total of All Dice	
4 of a Kind		Add Total of All Dice	
Full House		SCORE 25	
Sm. Straight	Sequence of 4	SCORE 30	
Lg. Straight	Sequence of 5	SCORE 40	
YAHTZEE	5 of a kind	SCORE 50	
Chance		Add Total of All 5 Dice	
YAHTZEE		✓ FOR EACH BONUS	
BONUS		SCORE 100 PER ✓	
TOTAL	Of Lower Section	⟶	
TOTAL	Of Upper Section	⟶	
GRAND TOTAL		⟶	

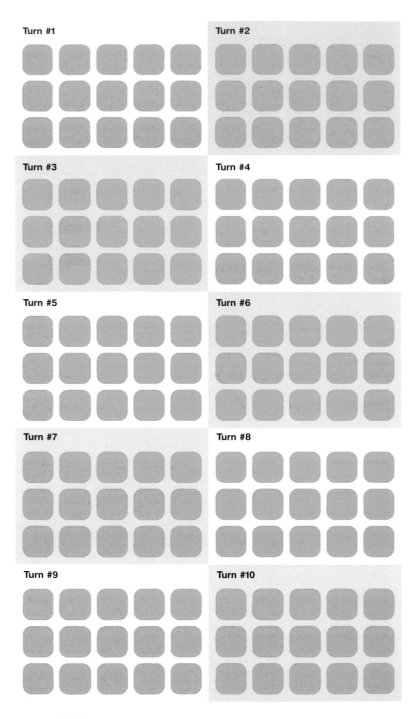

Turn #1

Turn #2

Turn #3

Turn #4

Turn #5

Turn #6

Turn #7

Turn #8

Turn #9

Turn #10

Turn #11

Turn #12

Turn #13

Can You Beat Pete?

Peter's score:

OSYP score:

Maximum score:

Your score: _____

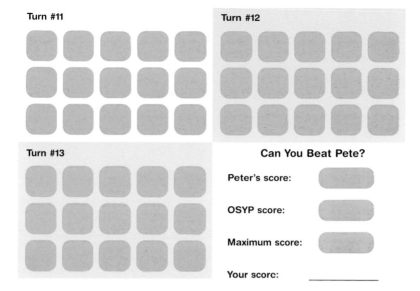

Yahtzee Scratch & Play

UPPER SECTION		HOW TO SCORE	SCORE
Aces	· = 1	Count and Add Only Aces	
Twos	: = 2	Count and Add Only Twos	
Threes	∴ = 3	Count and Add Only Threes	
Fours	:: = 4	Count and Add Only Fours	
Fives	⁙ = 5	Count and Add Only Fives	
Sixes	⁚⁚ = 6	Count and Add Only Sixes	
TOTAL SCORE		⟶	
BONUS	If total score is 63 or over	SCORE 35	
TOTAL	Of Upper Section	⟶	
LOWER SECTION			
3 of a Kind		Add Total of All Dice	
4 of a Kind		Add Total of All Dice	
Full House		SCORE 25	
Sm. Straight	Sequence of 4	SCORE 30	
Lg. Straight	Sequence of 5	SCORE 40	
YAHTZEE	5 of a kind	SCORE 50	
Chance		Add Total of All 5 Dice	
YAHTZEE BONUS		✓ FOR EACH BONUS	
		SCORE 100 PER ✓	
TOTAL	Of Lower Section	⟶	
TOTAL	Of Upper Section	⟶	
GRAND TOTAL		⟶	

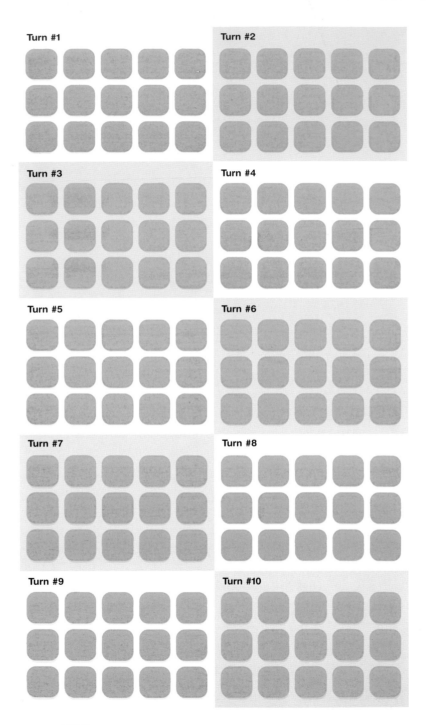

Turn #11

Turn #12

Turn #13

Can You Beat Pete?

Peter's score:

OSYP score:

Maximum score:

Your score: _____

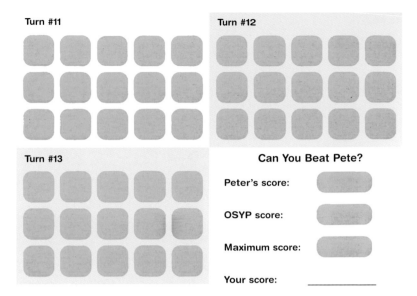

Scratch & Play

UPPER SECTION		HOW TO SCORE	SCORE
Aces	⊡ = 1	Count and Add Only Aces	
Twos	⊡ = 2	Count and Add Only Twos	
Threes	⊡ = 3	Count and Add Only Threes	
Fours	⊡ = 4	Count and Add Only Fours	
Fives	⊡ = 5	Count and Add Only Fives	
Sixes	⊡ = 6	Count and Add Only Sixes	
TOTAL SCORE		➝	
BONUS	If total score is 63 or over	SCORE 35	
TOTAL	Of Upper Section	➝	
LOWER SECTION			
3 of a Kind		Add Total of All Dice	
4 of a Kind		Add Total of All Dice	
Full House		SCORE 25	
Sm. Straight	Sequence of 4	SCORE 30	
Lg. Straight	Sequence of 5	SCORE 40	
YAHTZEE	5 of a kind	SCORE 50	
Chance		Add Total of All 5 Dice	
YAHTZEE BONUS		✓ FOR EACH BONUS	
		SCORE 100 PER ✓	
TOTAL	Of Lower Section	➝	
TOTAL	Of Upper Section	➝	
GRAND TOTAL		➝	

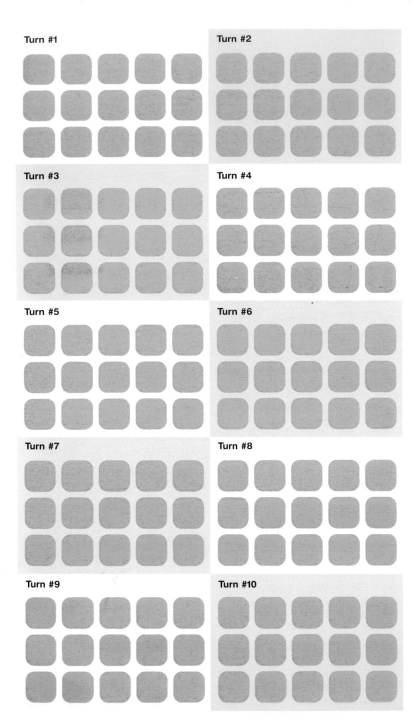

Turn #11

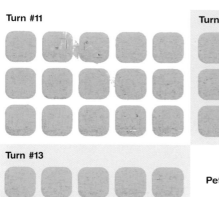

Turn #12

Turn #13

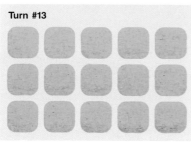

Can You Beat Pete?

Peter's score:

OSYP score:

Maximum score:

Your score: _____

Yahtzee Scratch & Play

UPPER SECTION		HOW TO SCORE	SCORE
Aces	· = 1	Count and Add Only Aces	
Twos	: = 2	Count and Add Only Twos	
Threes	∴ = 3	Count and Add Only Threes	
Fours	:: = 4	Count and Add Only Fours	
Fives	∷ = 5	Count and Add Only Fives	
Sixes	∷∷ = 6	Count and Add Only Sixes	
TOTAL SCORE		⟶	
BONUS	If total score is 63 or over	SCORE 35	
TOTAL	Of Upper Section	⟶	
LOWER SECTION			
3 of a Kind		Add Total of All Dice	
4 of a Kind		Add Total of All Dice	
Full House		SCORE 25	
Sm. Straight	Sequence of 4	SCORE 30	
Lg. Straight	Sequence of 5	SCORE 40	
YAHTZEE	5 of a kind	SCORE 50	
Chance		Add Total of All 5 Dice	
YAHTZEE BONUS		✓ FOR EACH BONUS	
		SCORE 100 PER ✓	
TOTAL	Of Lower Section	⟶	
TOTAL	Of Upper Section	⟶	
GRAND TOTAL		⟶	

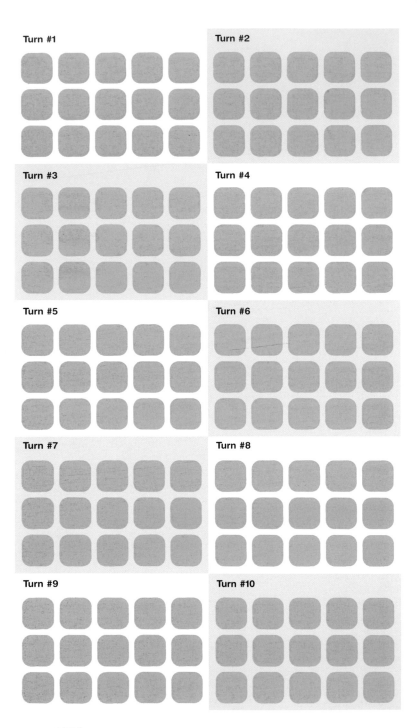

Turn #1

Turn #2

Turn #3

Turn #4

Turn #5

Turn #6

Turn #7

Turn #8

Turn #9

Turn #10

Turn #11

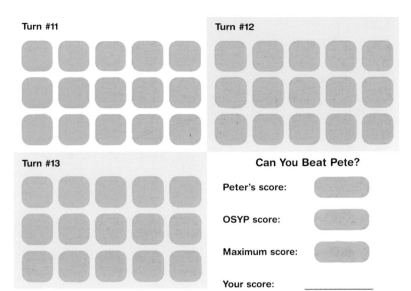

Turn #12

Turn #13

Can You Beat Pete?

Peter's score:

OSYP score:

Maximum score:

Your score: _____

Yahtzee Scratch & Play

UPPER SECTION		HOW TO SCORE	SCORE
Aces	⊡ = 1	Count and Add Only Aces	
Twos	⊡ = 2	Count and Add Only Twos	
Threes	⊡ = 3	Count and Add Only Threes	
Fours	⊡ = 4	Count and Add Only Fours	
Fives	⊡ = 5	Count and Add Only Fives	
Sixes	⊡ = 6	Count and Add Only Sixes	
TOTAL SCORE		⟶	
BONUS	If total score is 63 or over	SCORE 35	
TOTAL	Of Upper Section	⟶	
LOWER SECTION			
3 of a Kind		Add Total of All Dice	
4 of a Kind		Add Total of All Dice	
Full House		SCORE 25	
Sm. Straight	Sequence of 4	SCORE 30	
Lg. Straight	Sequence of 5	SCORE 40	
YAHTZEE	5 of a kind	SCORE 50	
Chance		Add Total of All 5 Dice	
YAHTZEE BONUS		✓ FOR EACH BONUS	
		SCORE 100 PER ✓	
TOTAL	Of Lower Section	⟶	
TOTAL	Of Upper Section	⟶	
GRAND TOTAL		⟶	

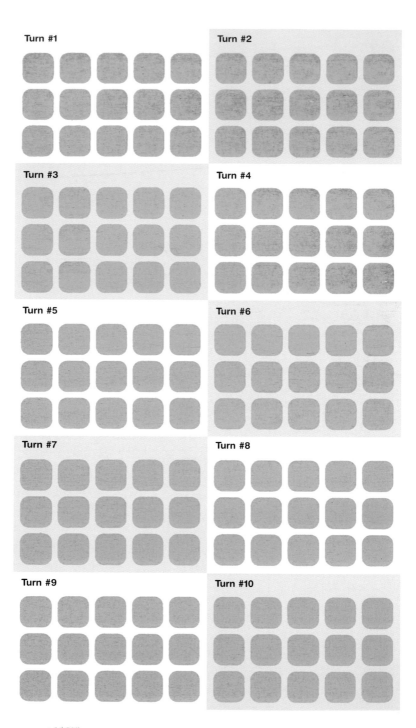

Turn #1

Turn #2

Turn #3

Turn #4

Turn #5

Turn #6

Turn #7

Turn #8

Turn #9

Turn #10

Turn #11

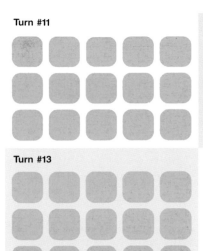

Turn #12

Turn #13

Can You Beat Pete?

Peter's score:

OSYP score:

Maximum score:

Your score: _____

Yahtzee Scratch & Play

UPPER SECTION		HOW TO SCORE	SCORE
Aces	• = 1	Count and Add Only Aces	
Twos	= 2	Count and Add Only Twos	
Threes	= 3	Count and Add Only Threes	
Fours	= 4	Count and Add Only Fours	
Fives	= 5	Count and Add Only Fives	
Sixes	= 6	Count and Add Only Sixes	
TOTAL SCORE		⟶	
BONUS	If total score is 63 or over	SCORE 35	
TOTAL	Of Upper Section	⟶	
LOWER SECTION			
3 of a Kind		Add Total of All Dice	
4 of a Kind		Add Total of All Dice	
Full House		SCORE 25	
Sm. Straight	Sequence of 4	SCORE 30	
Lg. Straight	Sequence of 5	SCORE 40	
YAHTZEE	5 of a kind	SCORE 50	
Chance		Add Total of All 5 Dice	
YAHTZEE BONUS		✓ FOR EACH BONUS	
		SCORE 100 PER ✓	
TOTAL	Of Lower Section	⟶	
TOTAL	Of Upper Section	⟶	
GRAND TOTAL		⟶	

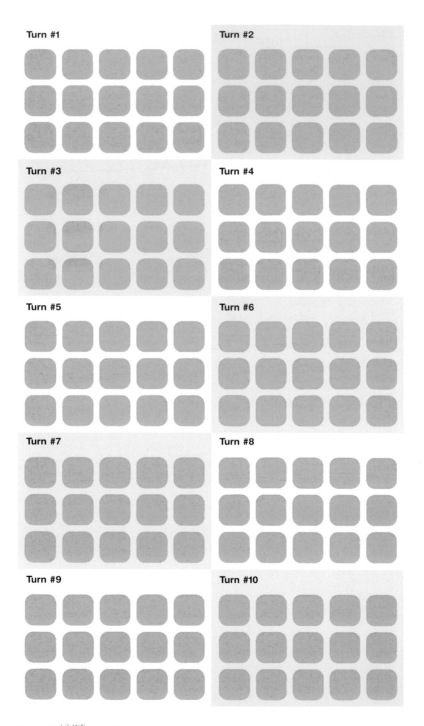

Turn #1

Turn #2

Turn #3

Turn #4

Turn #5

Turn #6

Turn #7

Turn #8

Turn #9

Turn #10

Turn #11

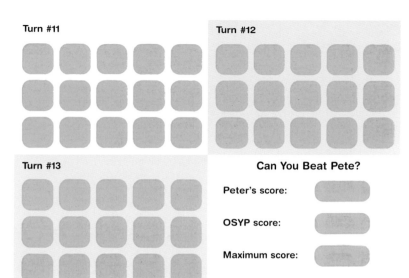

Turn #12

Turn #13

Can You Beat Pete?

Peter's score:

OSYP score:

Maximum score:

Your score: _____

~~Yahtzee~~ Scratch & Play

UPPER SECTION		HOW TO SCORE	SCORE
Aces	⚀ = 1	Count and Add Only Aces	
Twos	⚁ = 2	Count and Add Only Twos	
Threes	⚂ = 3	Count and Add Only Threes	
Fours	⚃ = 4	Count and Add Only Fours	
Fives	⚄ = 5	Count and Add Only Fives	
Sixes	⚅ = 6	Count and Add Only Sixes	
TOTAL SCORE		⟶	
BONUS	If total score is 63 or over	SCORE 35	
TOTAL	Of Upper Section	⟶	
LOWER SECTION			
3 of a Kind		Add Total of All Dice	
4 of a Kind		Add Total of All Dice	
Full House		SCORE 25	
Sm. Straight	Sequence of 4	SCORE 30	
Lg. Straight	Sequence of 5	SCORE 40	
YAHTZEE	5 of a kind	SCORE 50	
Chance		Add Total of All 5 Dice	
YAHTZEE BONUS		✓ FOR EACH BONUS	
		SCORE 100 PER ✓	
TOTAL	Of Lower Section	⟶	
TOTAL	Of Upper Section	⟶	
GRAND TOTAL		⟶	

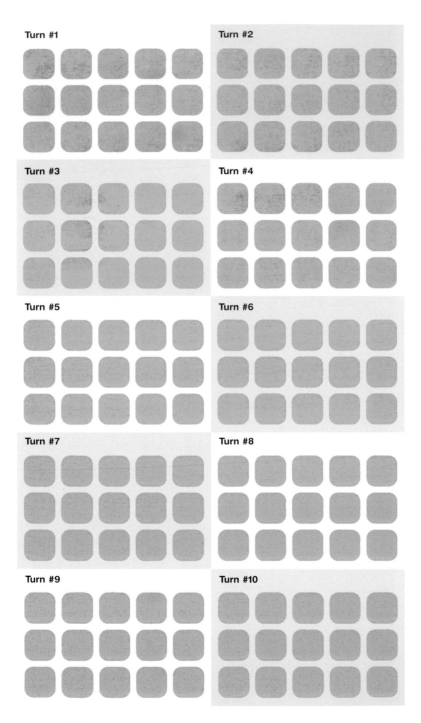

Turn #11

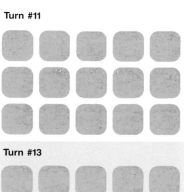

Turn #12

Turn #13

Can You Beat Pete?

Peter's score:

OSYP score:

Maximum score:

Your score: _____

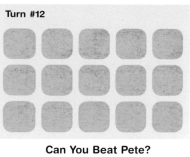

Yahtzee Scratch & Play

UPPER SECTION		HOW TO SCORE	SCORE
Aces	⚀ = 1	Count and Add Only Aces	
Twos	⚁ = 2	Count and Add Only Twos	
Threes	⚂ = 3	Count and Add Only Threes	
Fours	⚃ = 4	Count and Add Only Fours	
Fives	⚄ = 5	Count and Add Only Fives	
Sixes	⚅ = 6	Count and Add Only Sixes	
TOTAL SCORE		⟶	
BONUS	If total score is 63 or over	SCORE 35	
TOTAL	Of Upper Section	⟶	
LOWER SECTION			
3 of a Kind		Add Total of All Dice	
4 of a Kind		Add Total of All Dice	
Full House		SCORE 25	
Sm. Straight	Sequence of 4	SCORE 30	
Lg. Straight	Sequence of 5	SCORE 40	
YAHTZEE	5 of a kind	SCORE 50	
Chance		Add Total of All 5 Dice	
YAHTZEE BONUS		✓ FOR EACH BONUS	
		SCORE 100 PER ✓	
TOTAL	Of Lower Section	⟶	
TOTAL	Of Upper Section	⟶	
GRAND TOTAL		⟶	

Turn #1

Turn #2

Turn #3

Turn #4

Turn #5

Turn #6

Turn #7

Turn #8

Turn #9

Turn #10

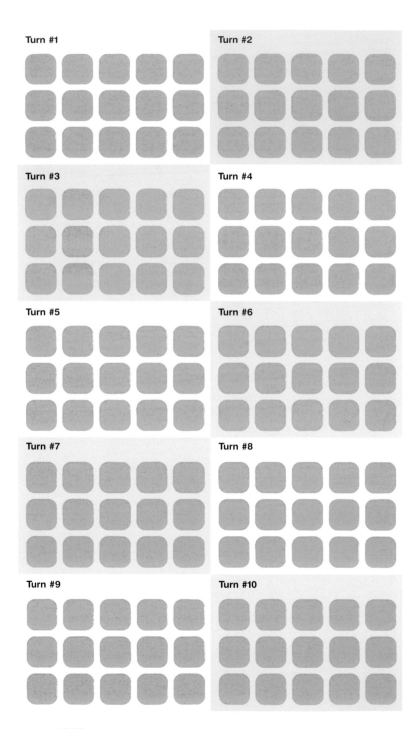

Turn #11

Turn #12

Turn #13

Can You Beat Pete?

Peter's score:

OSYP score:

Maximum score:

Your score: _____

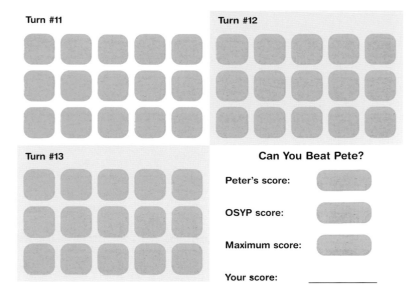

Yahtzee Scratch & Play

UPPER SECTION		HOW TO SCORE	SCORE
Aces	⋅ = 1	Count and Add Only Aces	
Twos	⋅⋅ = 2	Count and Add Only Twos	
Threes	⋅⋅⋅ = 3	Count and Add Only Threes	
Fours	⋅⋅⋅⋅ = 4	Count and Add Only Fours	
Fives	⋅⋅⋅⋅⋅ = 5	Count and Add Only Fives	
Sixes	⋅⋅⋅⋅⋅⋅ = 6	Count and Add Only Sixes	
TOTAL SCORE		⟶	
BONUS	If total score is 63 or over	SCORE 35	
TOTAL	Of Upper Section	⟶	
LOWER SECTION			
3 of a Kind		Add Total of All Dice	
4 of a Kind		Add Total of All Dice	
Full House		SCORE 25	
Sm. Straight	Sequence of 4	SCORE 30	
Lg. Straight	Sequence of 5	SCORE 40	
YAHTZEE	5 of a kind	SCORE 50	
Chance		Add Total of All 5 Dice	
YAHTZEE BONUS		✓ FOR EACH BONUS	
		SCORE 100 PER ✓	
TOTAL	Of Lower Section	⟶	
TOTAL	Of Upper Section	⟶	
GRAND TOTAL		⟶	

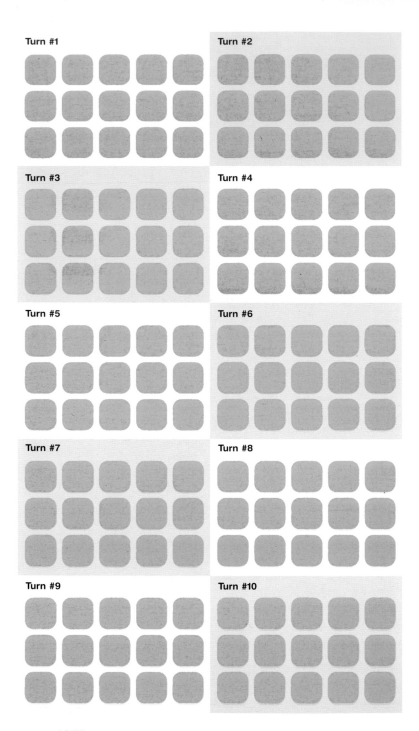

Turn #1

Turn #2

Turn #3

Turn #4

Turn #5

Turn #6

Turn #7

Turn #8

Turn #9

Turn #10

Turn #11

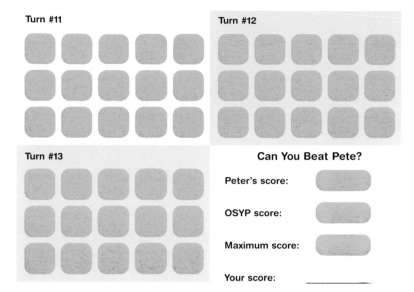

Turn #12

Turn #13

Can You Beat Pete?

Peter's score:

OSYP score:

Maximum score:

Your score:

Scratch & Play

UPPER SECTION		HOW TO SCORE	SCORE
Aces	▪ = 1	Count and Add Only Aces	
Twos	= 2	Count and Add Only Twos	
Threes	= 3	Count and Add Only Threes	
Fours	= 4	Count and Add Only Fours	
Fives	= 5	Count and Add Only Fives	
Sixes	= 6	Count and Add Only Sixes	
TOTAL SCORE		⟶	
BONUS	If total score is 63 or over	SCORE 35	
TOTAL	Of Upper Section	⟶	
LOWER SECTION			
3 of a Kind		Add Total of All Dice	
4 of a Kind		Add Total of All Dice	
Full House		SCORE 25	
Sm. Straight	Sequence of 4	SCORE 30	
Lg. Straight	Sequence of 5	SCORE 40	
YAHTZEE	5 of a kind	SCORE 50	
Chance		Add Total of All 5 Dice	
YAHTZEE BONUS		✓ FOR EACH BONUS	
		SCORE 100 PER ✓	
TOTAL	Of Lower Section	⟶	
TOTAL	Of Upper Section	⟶	
GRAND TOTAL		⟶	

Turn #1

Turn #2

Turn #3

Turn #4

Turn #5

Turn #6

Turn #7

Turn #8

Turn #9

Turn #10

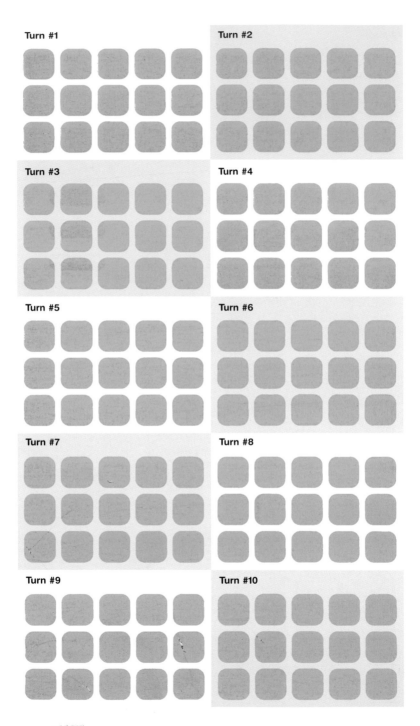

Turn #11

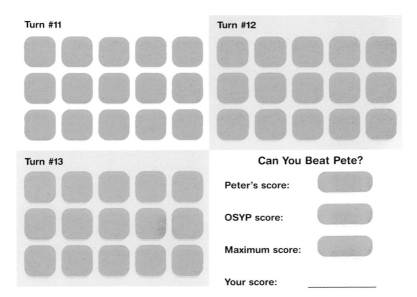

Turn #12

Turn #13

Can You Beat Pete?

Peter's score:

OSYP score:

Maximum score:

Your score: _____

Yahtzee Scratch & Play

UPPER SECTION		HOW TO SCORE	SCORE
Aces	⚀ = 1	Count and Add Only Aces	
Twos	⚁ = 2	Count and Add Only Twos	
Threes	⚂ = 3	Count and Add Only Threes	
Fours	⚃ = 4	Count and Add Only Fours	
Fives	⚄ = 5	Count and Add Only Fives	
Sixes	⚅ = 6	Count and Add Only Sixes	
TOTAL SCORE		⟶	
BONUS	If total score is 63 or over	SCORE 35	
TOTAL	Of Upper Section	⟶	
LOWER SECTION			
3 of a Kind		Add Total of All Dice	
4 of a Kind		Add Total of All Dice	
Full House		SCORE 25	
Sm. Straight	Sequence of 4	SCORE 30	
Lg. Straight	Sequence of 5	SCORE 40	
YAHTZEE	5 of a kind	SCORE 50	
Chance		Add Total of All 5 Dice	
YAHTZEE BONUS		✓ FOR EACH BONUS	
		SCORE 100 PER ✓	
TOTAL	Of Lower Section	⟶	
TOTAL	Of Upper Section	⟶	
GRAND TOTAL		⟶	

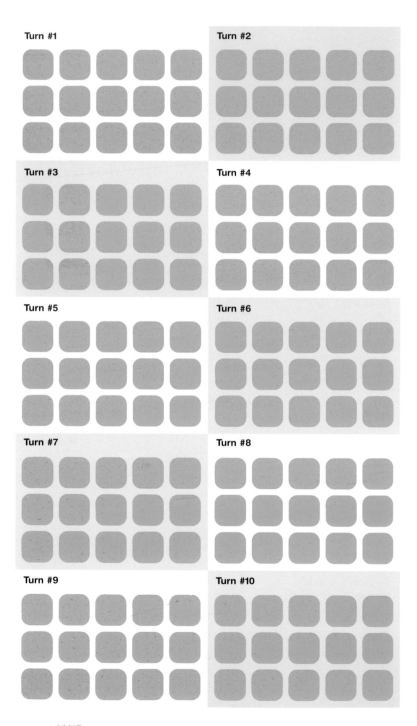

Turn #1

Turn #2

Turn #3

Turn #4

Turn #5

Turn #6

Turn #7

Turn #8

Turn #9

Turn #10

Turn #11

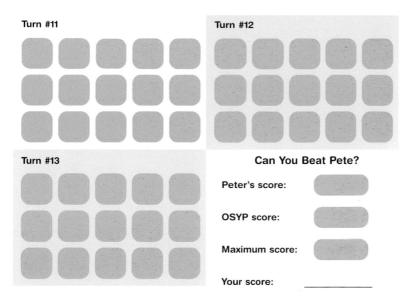

Turn #12

Turn #13

Can You Beat Pete?

Peter's score:

OSYP score:

Maximum score:

Your score: _____

Scratch & Play

UPPER SECTION		HOW TO SCORE	SCORE
Aces	⚀ = 1	Count and Add Only Aces	
Twos	⚁ = 2	Count and Add Only Twos	
Threes	⚂ = 3	Count and Add Only Threes	
Fours	⚃ = 4	Count and Add Only Fours	
Fives	⚄ = 5	Count and Add Only Fives	
Sixes	⚅ = 6	Count and Add Only Sixes	
TOTAL SCORE		➡	
BONUS	If total score is 63 or over	SCORE 35	
TOTAL	Of Upper Section	➡	
LOWER SECTION			
3 of a Kind		Add Total of All Dice	
4 of a Kind		Add Total of All Dice	
Full House		SCORE 25	
Sm. Straight	Sequence of 4	SCORE 30	
Lg. Straight	Sequence of 5	SCORE 40	
YAHTZEE	5 of a kind	SCORE 50	
Chance		Add Total of All 5 Dice	
YAHTZEE BONUS		✓ FOR EACH BONUS	
		SCORE 100 PER ✓	
TOTAL	Of Lower Section	➡	
TOTAL	Of Upper Section	➡	
GRAND TOTAL		➡	

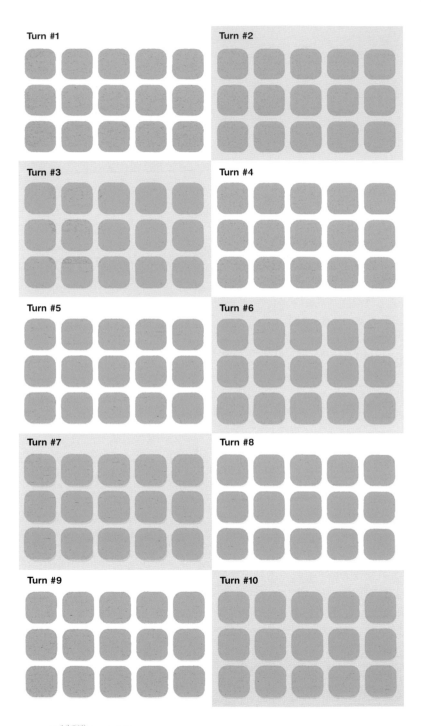

Turn #1

Turn #2

Turn #3

Turn #4

Turn #5

Turn #6

Turn #7

Turn #8

Turn #9

Turn #10

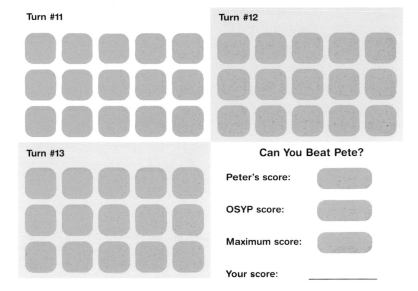

Turn #11

Turn #12

Turn #13

Can You Beat Pete?

Peter's score:

OSYP score:

Maximum score:

Your score: _____

Yahtzee Scratch & Play

UPPER SECTION		HOW TO SCORE	SCORE
Aces	⚀ = 1	Count and Add Only Aces	
Twos	⚁ = 2	Count and Add Only Twos	
Threes	⚂ = 3	Count and Add Only Threes	
Fours	⚃ = 4	Count and Add Only Fours	
Fives	⚄ = 5	Count and Add Only Fives	
Sixes	⚅ = 6	Count and Add Only Sixes	
TOTAL SCORE		➡	
BONUS	If total score is 63 or over	SCORE 35	
TOTAL	Of Upper Section	➡	
LOWER SECTION			
3 of a Kind		Add Total of All Dice	
4 of a Kind		Add Total of All Dice	
Full House		SCORE 25	
Sm. Straight	Sequence of 4	SCORE 30	
Lg. Straight	Sequence of 5	SCORE 40	
YAHTZEE	5 of a kind	SCORE 50	
Chance		Add Total of All 5 Dice	
YAHTZEE BONUS		✓ FOR EACH BONUS	
		SCORE 100 PER ✓	
TOTAL	Of Lower Section	➡	
TOTAL	Of Upper Section	➡	
GRAND TOTAL		➡	

Turn #1

Turn #2

Turn #3

Turn #4

Turn #5

Turn #6

Turn #7

Turn #8

Turn #9

Turn #10

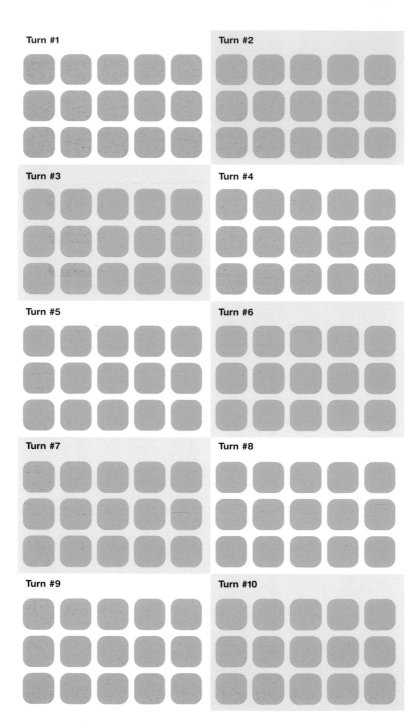

Turn #11

Turn #12

Turn #13

Can You Beat Pete?

Peter's score:

OSYP score:

Maximum score:

Your score: _____

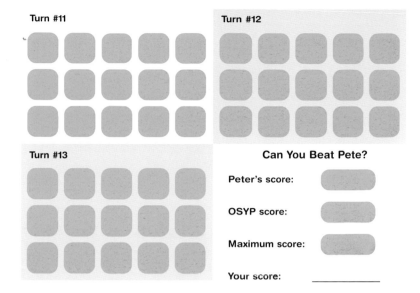

Scratch & Play

UPPER SECTION		HOW TO SCORE	SCORE
Aces	⚀ = 1	Count and Add Only Aces	
Twos	⚁ = 2	Count and Add Only Twos	
Threes	⚂ = 3	Count and Add Only Threes	
Fours	⚃ = 4	Count and Add Only Fours	
Fives	⚄ = 5	Count and Add Only Fives	
Sixes	⚅ = 6	Count and Add Only Sixes	
TOTAL SCORE		➜	
BONUS	If total score is 63 or over	SCORE 35	
TOTAL	Of Upper Section	➜	
LOWER SECTION			
3 of a Kind		Add Total of All Dice	
4 of a Kind		Add Total of All Dice	
Full House		SCORE 25	
Sm. Straight	Sequence of 4	SCORE 30	
Lg. Straight	Sequence of 5	SCORE 40	
YAHTZEE	5 of a kind	SCORE 50	
Chance		Add Total of All 5 Dice	
YAHTZEE BONUS		✓ FOR EACH BONUS	
		SCORE 100 PER ✓	
TOTAL	Of Lower Section	➜	
TOTAL	Of Upper Section	➜	
GRAND TOTAL		➜	

Turn #1

Turn #2

Turn #3

Turn #4

Turn #5

Turn #6

Turn #7

Turn #8

Turn #9

Turn #10

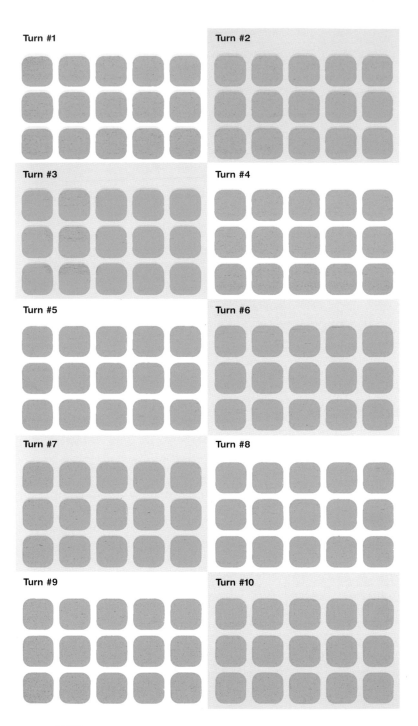

Turn #11

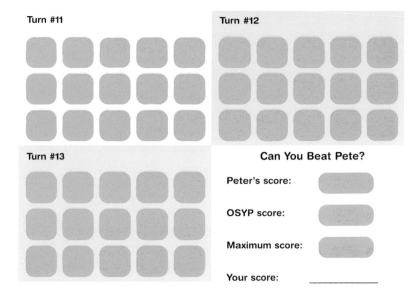

Turn #12

Turn #13

Can You Beat Pete?

Peter's score:

OSYP score:

Maximum score:

Your score: _____

Yahtzee Scratch & Play

UPPER SECTION		HOW TO SCORE	SCORE
Aces	⚀ = 1	Count and Add Only Aces	
Twos	⚁ = 2	Count and Add Only Twos	
Threes	⚂ = 3	Count and Add Only Threes	
Fours	⚃ = 4	Count and Add Only Fours	
Fives	⚄ = 5	Count and Add Only Fives	
Sixes	⚅ = 6	Count and Add Only Sixes	
TOTAL SCORE		⟶	
BONUS	If total score is 63 or over	SCORE 35	
TOTAL	Of Upper Section	⟶	
LOWER SECTION			
3 of a Kind		Add Total of All Dice	
4 of a Kind		Add Total of All Dice	
Full House		SCORE 25	
Sm. Straight	Sequence of 4	SCORE 30	
Lg. Straight	Sequence of 5	SCORE 40	
YAHTZEE	5 of a kind	SCORE 50	
Chance		Add Total of All 5 Dice	
YAHTZEE BONUS		✓ FOR EACH BONUS	
		SCORE 100 PER ✓	
TOTAL	Of Lower Section	⟶	
TOTAL	Of Upper Section	⟶	
GRAND TOTAL		⟶	

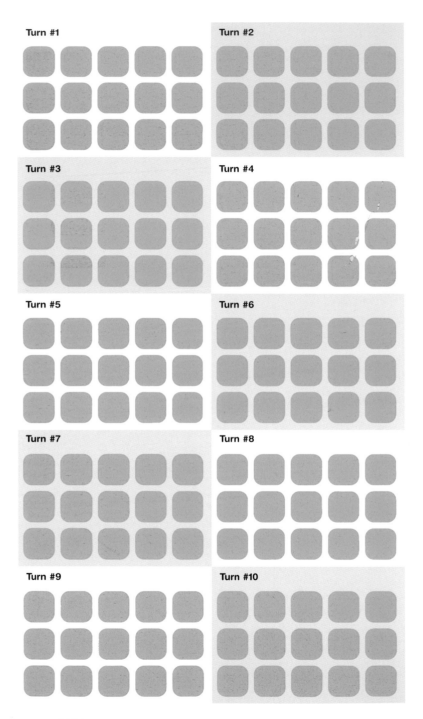

Turn #1

Turn #2

Turn #3

Turn #4

Turn #5

Turn #6

Turn #7

Turn #8

Turn #9

Turn #10

Turn #11

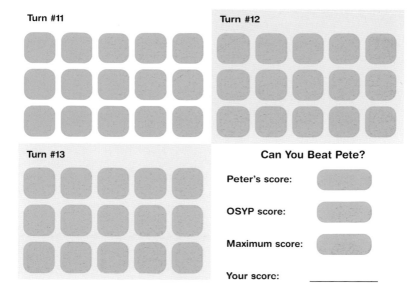

Turn #12

Turn #13

Can You Beat Pete?

Peter's score:

OSYP score:

Maximum score:

Your score: _____

Yahtzee Scratch & Play

UPPER SECTION		HOW TO SCORE	SCORE
Aces	⚀ = 1	Count and Add Only Aces	
Twos	⚁ = 2	Count and Add Only Twos	
Threes	⚂ = 3	Count and Add Only Threes	
Fours	⚃ = 4	Count and Add Only Fours	
Fives	⚄ = 5	Count and Add Only Fives	
Sixes	⚅ = 6	Count and Add Only Sixes	
TOTAL SCORE		➔	
BONUS	If total score is 63 or over	SCORE 35	
TOTAL	Of Upper Section	➔	
LOWER SECTION			
3 of a Kind		Add Total of All Dice	
4 of a Kind		Add Total of All Dice	
Full House		SCORE 25	
Sm. Straight	Sequence of 4	SCORE 30	
Lg. Straight	Sequence of 5	SCORE 40	
YAHTZEE	5 of a kind	SCORE 50	
Chance		Add Total of All 5 Dice	
YAHTZEE BONUS		✓ FOR EACH BONUS	
		SCORE 100 PER ✓	
TOTAL	Of Lower Section	➔	
TOTAL	Of Upper Section	➔	
GRAND TOTAL		➔	

Turn #1

Turn #2

Turn #3

Turn #4

Turn #5

Turn #6

Turn #7

Turn #8

Turn #9

Turn #10

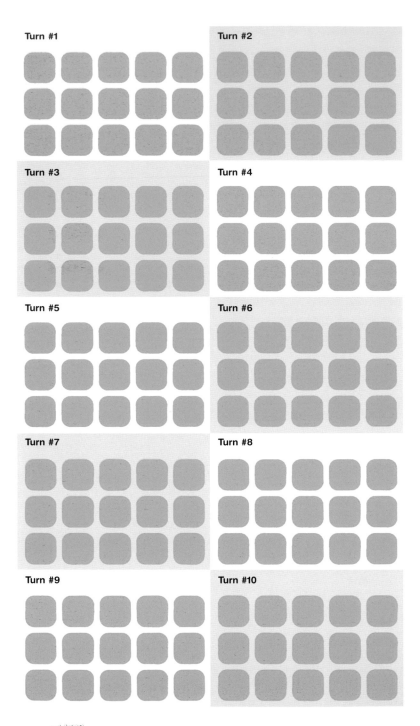

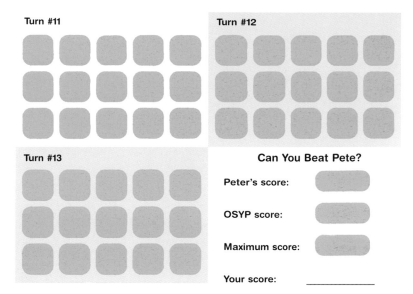

Turn #11

Turn #12

Turn #13

Can You Beat Pete?

Peter's score:

OSYP score:

Maximum score:

Your score: _____

Yahtzee Scratch & Play

UPPER SECTION	HOW TO SCORE	SCORE
Aces · = 1	Count and Add Only Aces	
Twos ·· = 2	Count and Add Only Twos	
Threes ·· = 3	Count and Add Only Threes	
Fours :: = 4	Count and Add Only Fours	
Fives ·:· = 5	Count and Add Only Fives	
Sixes ::: = 6	Count and Add Only Sixes	
TOTAL SCORE	⟶	
BONUS If total score is 63 or over	SCORE 35	
TOTAL Of Upper Section	⟶	
LOWER SECTION		
3 of a Kind	Add Total of All Dice	
4 of a Kind	Add Total of All Dice	
Full House	SCORE 25	
Sm. Straight Sequence of 4	SCORE 30	
Lg. Straight Sequence of 5	SCORE 40	
YAHTZEE 5 of a kind	SCORE 50	
Chance	Add Total of All 5 Dice	
YAHTZEE BONUS	✓ FOR EACH BONUS	
	SCORE 100 PER ✓	
TOTAL Of Lower Section	⟶	
TOTAL Of Upper Section	⟶	
GRAND TOTAL	⟶	

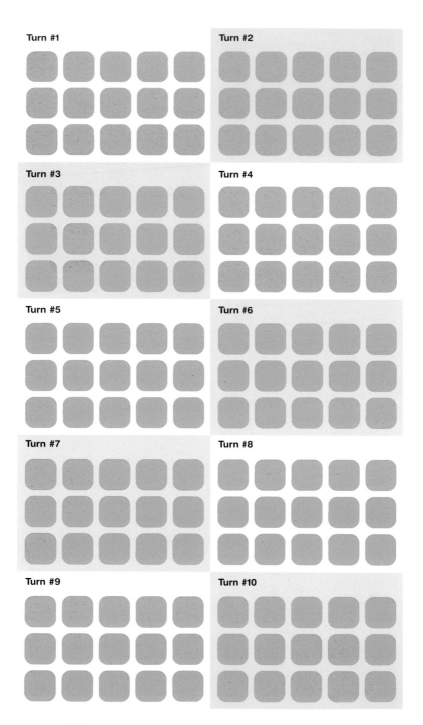

Turn #1

Turn #2

Turn #3

Turn #4

Turn #5

Turn #6

Turn #7

Turn #8

Turn #9

Turn #10

Turn #11

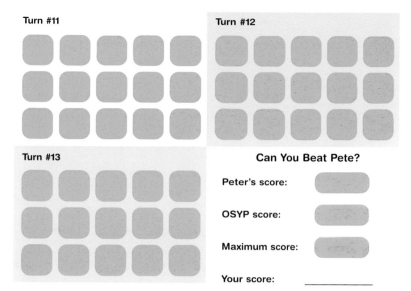

Turn #12

Turn #13

Can You Beat Pete?

Peter's score:

OSYP score:

Maximum score:

Your score: _____

Yahtzee Scratch & Play

UPPER SECTION		HOW TO SCORE	SCORE
Aces	⚀ = 1	Count and Add Only Aces	
Twos	⚁ = 2	Count and Add Only Twos	
Threes	⚂ − 3	Count and Add Only Threes	
Fours	⚃ = 4	Count and Add Only Fours	
Fives	⚄ = 5	Count and Add Only Fives	
Sixes	⚅ = 6	Count and Add Only Sixes	
TOTAL SCORE		⟶	
BONUS	If total score is 63 or over	SCORE 35	
TOTAL	Of Upper Section	⟶	
LOWER SECTION			
3 of a Kind		Add Total of All Dice	
4 of a Kind		Add Total of All Dice	
Full House		SCORE 25	
Sm. Straight	Sequence of 4	SCORE 30	
Lg. Straight	Sequence of 5	SCORE 40	
YAHTZEE	5 of a kind	SCORE 50	
Chance		Add Total of All 5 Dice	
YAHTZEE BONUS		✓ FOR EACH BONUS	
		SCORE 100 PER ✓	
TOTAL	Of Lower Section	⟶	
TOTAL	Of Upper Section	⟶	
GRAND TOTAL		⟶	

Turn #1

Turn #2

Turn #3

Turn #4

Turn #5

Turn #6

Turn #7

Turn #8

Turn #9

Turn #10

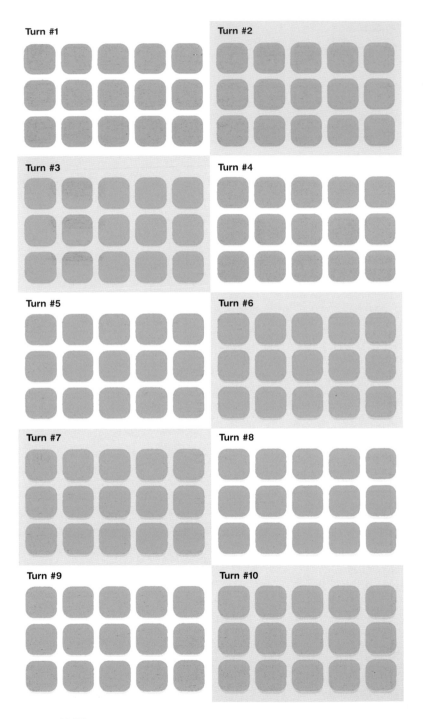

Turn #11

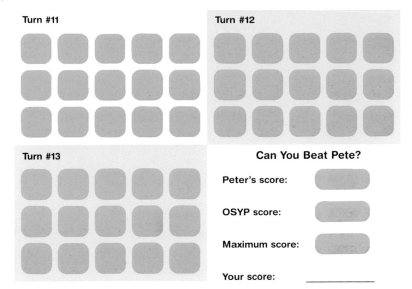

Turn #12

Turn #13

Can You Beat Pete?

Peter's score:

OSYP score:

Maximum score:

Your score: _____

Yahtzee Scratch & Play

UPPER SECTION		HOW TO SCORE	SCORE
Aces	• = 1	Count and Add Only Aces	
Twos	•• = 2	Count and Add Only Twos	
Threes	•.• = 3	Count and Add Only Threes	
Fours	:: = 4	Count and Add Only Fours	
Fives	•:• = 5	Count and Add Only Fives	
Sixes	::: = 6	Count and Add Only Sixes	
TOTAL SCORE		⟶	
BONUS	If total score is 63 or over	SCORE 35	
TOTAL	Of Upper Section	⟶	
LOWER SECTION			
3 of a Kind		Add Total of All Dice	
4 of a Kind		Add Total of All Dice	
Full House		SCORE 25	
Sm. Straight	Sequence of 4	SCORE 30	
Lg. Straight	Sequence of 5	SCORE 40	
YAHTZEE	5 of a kind	SCORE 50	
Chance		Add Total of All 5 Dice	
YAHTZEE BONUS		✓ FOR EACH BONUS	
		SCORE 100 PER ✓	
TOTAL	Of Lower Section	⟶	
TOTAL	Of Upper Section	⟶	
GRAND TOTAL		⟶	

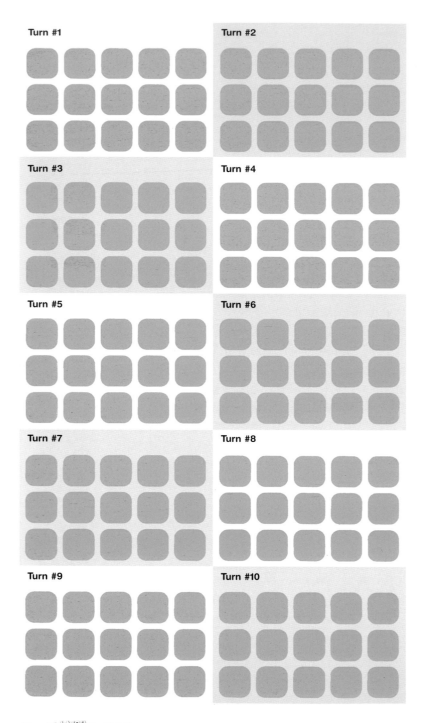

Turn #1

Turn #2

Turn #3

Turn #4

Turn #5

Turn #6

Turn #7

Turn #8

Turn #9

Turn #10

Turn #11

Turn #12

Turn #13

Can You Beat Pete?

Peter's score:

OSYP score:

Maximum score:

Your score: _____

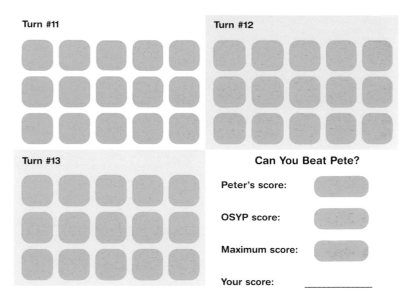

Scratch & Play

UPPER SECTION		HOW TO SCORE	SCORE
Aces	⊡ = 1	Count and Add Only Aces	
Twos	⊡ = 2	Count and Add Only Twos	
Threes	⊡ = 3	Count and Add Only Threes	
Fours	⊡ = 4	Count and Add Only Fours	
Fives	⊡ = 5	Count and Add Only Fives	
Sixes	⊞ = 6	Count and Add Only Sixes	
TOTAL SCORE		⟶	
BONUS	If total score is 63 or over	SCORE 35	
TOTAL	Of Upper Section	⟶	
LOWER SECTION			
3 of a Kind		Add Total of All Dice	
4 of a Kind		Add Total of All Dice	
Full House		SCORE 25	
Sm. Straight	Sequence of 4	SCORE 30	
Lg. Straight	Sequence of 5	SCORE 40	
YAHTZEE	5 of a kind	SCORE 50	
Chance		Add Total of All 5 Dice	
YAHTZEE BONUS		✓ FOR EACH BONUS	
		SCORE 100 PER ✓	
TOTAL	Of Lower Section	⟶	
TOTAL	Of Upper Section	⟶	
GRAND TOTAL		⟶	

Turn #1

Turn #2

Turn #3

Turn #4

Turn #5

Turn #6

Turn #7

Turn #8

Turn #9

Turn #10

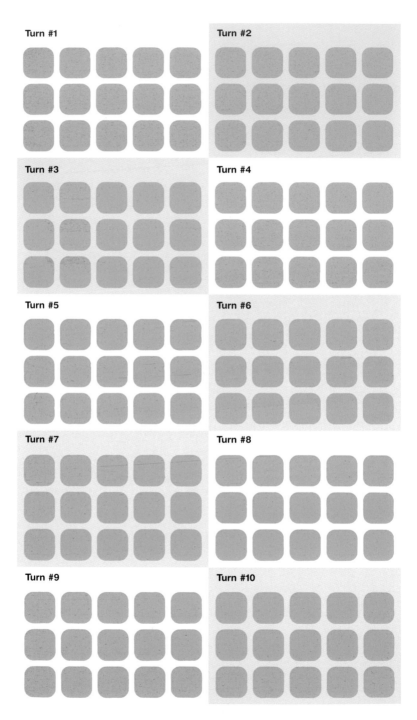

Turn #11

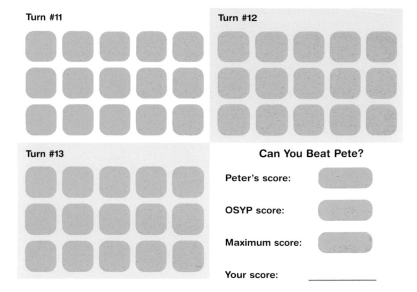

Turn #12

Turn #13

Can You Beat Pete?

Peter's score:

OSYP score:

Maximum score:

Your score: _____

Yahtzee Scratch & Play

UPPER SECTION		HOW TO SCORE	SCORE
Aces	⚀ = 1	Count and Add Only Aces	
Twos	⚁ = 2	Count and Add Only Twos	
Threes	⚂ = 3	Count and Add Only Threes	
Fours	⚃ = 4	Count and Add Only Fours	
Fives	⚄ = 5	Count and Add Only Fives	
Sixes	⚅ = 6	Count and Add Only Sixes	
TOTAL SCORE		➜	
BONUS	If total score is 63 or over	SCORE 35	
TOTAL	Of Upper Section	➜	
LOWER SECTION			
3 of a Kind		Add Total of All Dice	
4 of a Kind		Add Total of All Dice	
Full House		SCORE 25	
Sm. Straight	Sequence of 4	SCORE 30	
Lg. Straight	Sequence of 5	SCORE 40	
YAHTZEE	5 of a kind	SCORE 50	
Chance		Add Total of All 5 Dice	
YAHTZEE BONUS		✓ FOR EACH BONUS	
		SCORE 100 PER ✓	
TOTAL	Of Lower Section	➜	
TOTAL	Of Upper Section	➜	
GRAND TOTAL		➜	

Turn #1

Turn #2

Turn #3

Turn #4

Turn #5

Turn #6

Turn #7

Turn #8

Turn #9

Turn #10

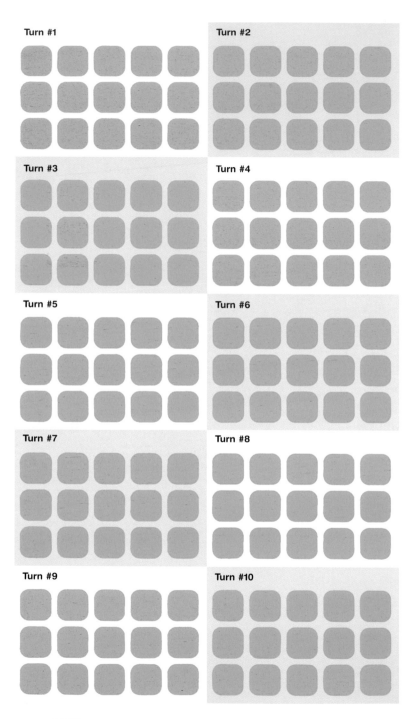

Turn #11

Turn #12

Turn #13

Can You Beat Pete?

Peter's score:

OSYP score:

Maximum score:

Your score: _____

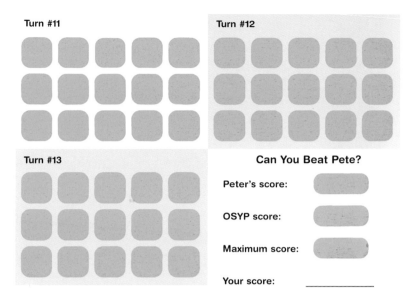

Scratch & Play

UPPER SECTION		HOW TO SCORE	SCORE
Aces	⚀ = 1	Count and Add Only Aces	
Twos	⚁ = 2	Count and Add Only Twos	
Threes	⚂ = 3	Count and Add Only Threes	
Fours	⚃ = 4	Count and Add Only Fours	
Fives	⚄ = 5	Count and Add Only Fives	
Sixes	⚅ = 6	Count and Add Only Sixes	
TOTAL SCORE		⟶	
BONUS	If total score is 63 or over	SCORE 35	
TOTAL	Of Upper Section	⟶	
LOWER SECTION			
3 of a Kind		Add Total of All Dice	
4 of a Kind		Add Total of All Dice	
Full House		SCORE 25	
Sm. Straight	Sequence of 4	SCORE 30	
Lg. Straight	Sequence of 5	SCORE 40	
YAHTZEE	5 of a kind	SCORE 50	
Chance		Add Total of All 5 Dice	
YAHTZEE BONUS		✓ FOR EACH BONUS	
		SCORE 100 PER ✓	
TOTAL	Of Lower Section	⟶	
TOTAL	Of Upper Section	⟶	
GRAND TOTAL		⟶	

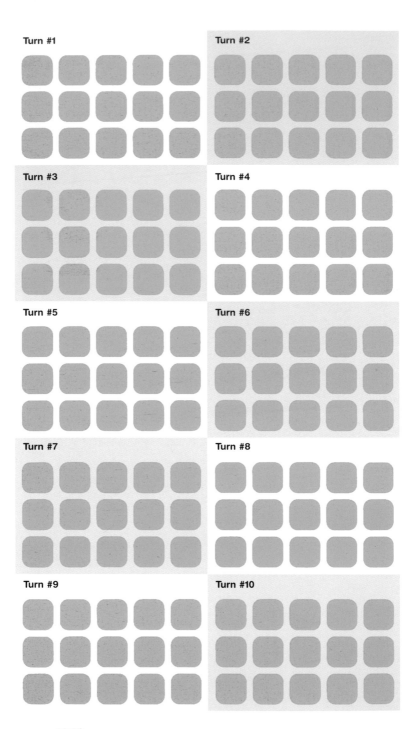

Turn #1

Turn #2

Turn #3

Turn #4

Turn #5

Turn #6

Turn #7

Turn #8

Turn #9

Turn #10

yahtzee Scratch & Play

Turn #11

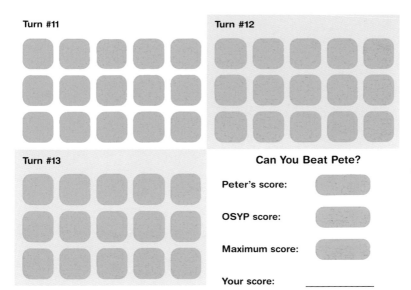

Turn #12

Turn #13

Can You Beat Pete?

Peter's score:

OSYP score:

Maximum score:

Your score: _____

Scratch & Play

UPPER SECTION		HOW TO SCORE	SCORE
Aces	⚀ = 1	Count and Add Only Aces	
Twos	⚁ = 2	Count and Add Only Twos	
Threes	⚂ = 3	Count and Add Only Threes	
Fours	⚃ = 4	Count and Add Only Fours	
Fives	⚄ = 5	Count and Add Only Fives	
Sixes	⚅ = 6	Count and Add Only Sixes	
TOTAL SCORE		⟶	
BONUS	If total score is 63 or over	SCORE 35	
TOTAL	Of Upper Section	⟶	
LOWER SECTION			
3 of a Kind		Add Total of All Dice	
4 of a Kind		Add Total of All Dice	
Full House		SCORE 25	
Sm. Straight	Sequence of 4	SCORE 30	
Lg. Straight	Sequence of 5	SCORE 40	
YAHTZEE	5 of a kind	SCORE 50	
Chance		Add Total of All 5 Dice	
YAHTZEE BONUS		✓ FOR EACH BONUS	
		SCORE 100 PER ✓	
TOTAL	Of Lower Section	⟶	
TOTAL	Of Upper Section	⟶	
GRAND TOTAL		⟶	

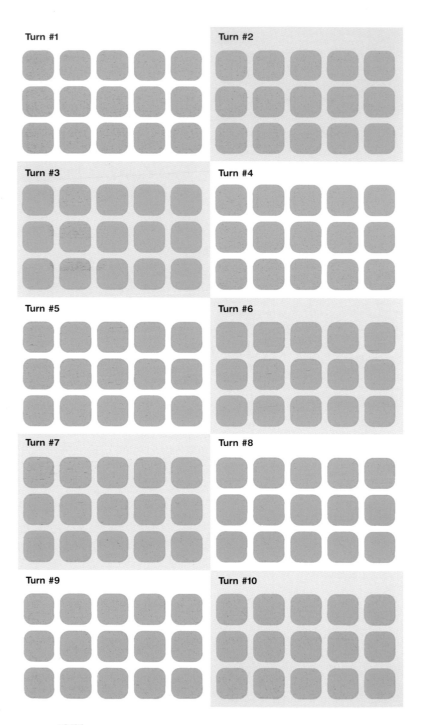

Turn #1

Turn #2

Turn #3

Turn #4

Turn #5

Turn #6

Turn #7

Turn #8

Turn #9

Turn #10

Turn #11

Turn #12

Turn #13

Can You Beat Pete?

Peter's score:

OSYP score:

Maximum score:

Your score: _____

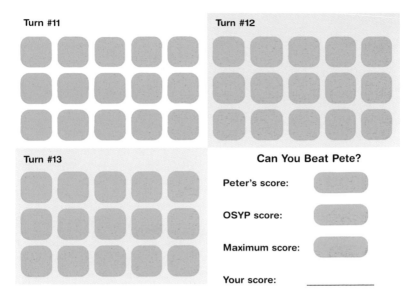

Scratch & Play

UPPER SECTION		HOW TO SCORE	SCORE
Aces	· = 1	Count and Add Only Aces	
Twos	·· = 2	Count and Add Only Twos	
Threes	∴ = 3	Count and Add Only Threes	
Fours	∷ = 4	Count and Add Only Fours	
Fives	⁙ = 5	Count and Add Only Fives	
Sixes	⊞ = 6	Count and Add Only Sixes	
TOTAL SCORE		⟶	
BONUS	If total score is 63 or over	SCORE 35	
TOTAL	Of Upper Section	⟶	
LOWER SECTION			
3 of a Kind		Add Total of All Dice	
4 of a Kind		Add Total of All Dice	
Full House		SCORE 25	
Sm. Straight	Sequence of 4	SCORE 30	
Lg. Straight	Sequence of 5	SCORE 40	
YAHTZEE	5 of a kind	SCORE 50	
Chance		Add Total of All 5 Dice	
YAHTZEE BONUS		✓ FOR EACH BONUS	
		SCORE 100 PER ✓	
TOTAL	Of Lower Section	⟶	
TOTAL	Of Upper Section	⟶	
GRAND TOTAL		⟶	

Turn #1

Turn #2

Turn #3

Turn #4

Turn #5

Turn #6

Turn #7

Turn #8

Turn #9

Turn #10

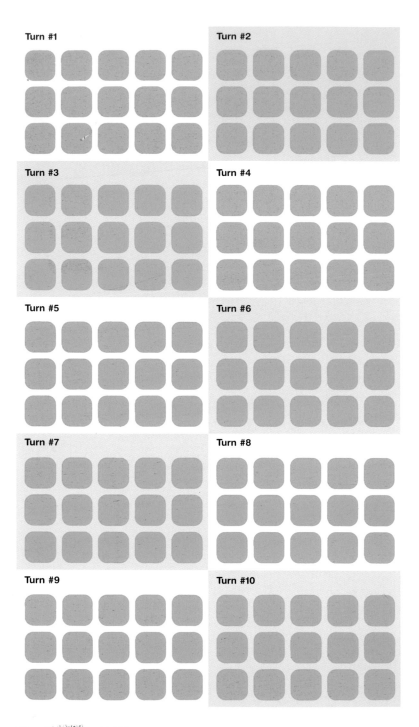

Turn #11

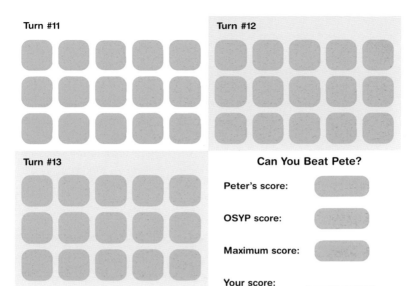

Turn #12

Turn #13

Can You Beat Pete?

Peter's score:

OSYP score:

Maximum score:

Your score: _____

ⓎⓐⓗⓉⓏⓔⓔ Scratch & Play

UPPER SECTION		HOW TO SCORE	SCORE
Aces	⊡ = 1	Count and Add Only Aces	
Twos	⊡ = 2	Count and Add Only Twos	
Threes	⊡ = 3	Count and Add Only Threes	
Fours	⊡ = 4	Count and Add Only Fours	
Fives	⊡ = 5	Count and Add Only Fives	
Sixes	⊞ = 6	Count and Add Only Sixes	
TOTAL SCORE		⟶	
BONUS	If total score is 63 or over	SCORE 35	
TOTAL	Of Upper Section	⟶	
LOWER SECTION			
3 of a Kind		Add Total of All Dice	
4 of a Kind		Add Total of All Dice	
Full House		SCORE 25	
Sm. Straight	Sequence of 4	SCORE 30	
Lg. Straight	Sequence of 5	SCORE 40	
YAHTZEE	5 of a kind	SCORE 50	
Chance		Add Total of All 5 Dice	
YAHTZEE BONUS		✓ FOR EACH BONUS	
		SCORE 100 PER ✓	
TOTAL	Of Lower Section	⟶	
TOTAL	Of Upper Section	⟶	
GRAND TOTAL		⟶	

Turn #1

Turn #2

Turn #3

Turn #4

Turn #5

Turn #6

Turn #7

Turn #8

Turn #9

Turn #10

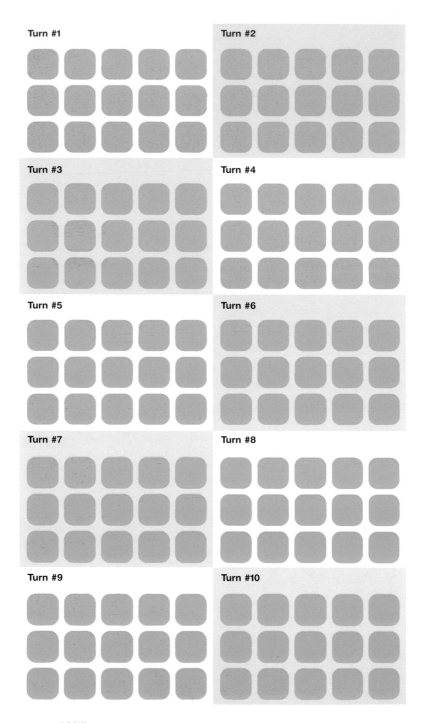

Turn #11

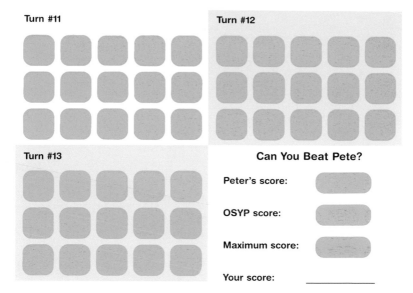

Turn #12

Turn #13

Can You Beat Pete?

Peter's score:

OSYP score:

Maximum score:

Your score: _____

Yahtzee Scratch & Play

UPPER SECTION		HOW TO SCORE	SCORE
Aces	⚀ = 1	Count and Add Only Aces	
Twos	⚁ = 2	Count and Add Only Twos	
Threes	⚂ = 3	Count and Add Only Threes	
Fours	⚃ = 4	Count and Add Only Fours	
Fives	⚄ = 5	Count and Add Only Fives	
Sixes	⚅ = 6	Count and Add Only Sixes	
TOTAL SCORE		⟶	
BONUS	If total score is 63 or over	SCORE 35	
TOTAL	Of Upper Section	⟶	
LOWER SECTION			
3 of a Kind		Add Total of All Dice	
4 of a Kind		Add Total of All Dice	
Full House		SCORE 25	
Sm. Straight	Sequence of 4	SCORE 30	
Lg. Straight	Sequence of 5	SCORE 40	
YAHTZEE	5 of a kind	SCORE 50	
Chance		Add Total of All 5 Dice	
YAHTZEE BONUS		✓ FOR EACH BONUS	
		SCORE 100 PER ✓	
TOTAL	Of Lower Section	⟶	
TOTAL	Of Upper Section	⟶	
GRAND TOTAL		⟶	

Turn #1

Turn #2

Turn #3

Turn #4

Turn #5

Turn #6

Turn #7

Turn #8

Turn #9

Turn #10

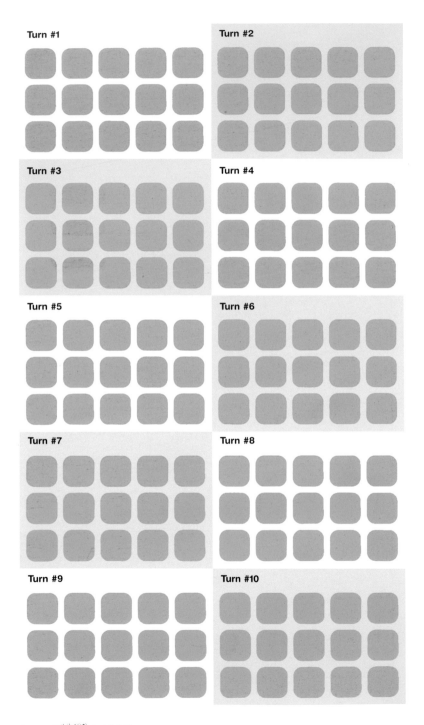

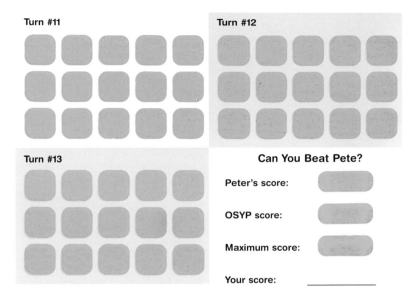

Turn #11

Turn #12

Turn #13

Can You Beat Pete?

Peter's score:

OSYP score:

Maximum score:

Your score: _____

Yahtzee Scratch & Play

UPPER SECTION		HOW TO SCORE	SCORE
Aces	⚀ = 1	Count and Add Only Aces	
Twos	⚁ = 2	Count and Add Only Twos	
Threes	⚂ = 3	Count and Add Only Threes	
Fours	⚃ = 4	Count and Add Only Fours	
Fives	⚄ = 5	Count and Add Only Fives	
Sixes	⚅ = 6	Count and Add Only Sixes	
TOTAL SCORE		➡	
BONUS	If total score is 63 or over	SCORE 35	
TOTAL	Of Upper Section	➡	
LOWER SECTION			
3 of a Kind		Add Total of All Dice	
4 of a Kind		Add Total of All Dice	
Full House		SCORE 25	
Sm. Straight	Sequence of 4	SCORE 30	
Lg. Straight	Sequence of 5	SCORE 40	
YAHTZEE	5 of a kind	SCORE 50	
Chance		Add Total of All 5 Dice	
YAHTZEE BONUS		✓ FOR EACH BONUS	
		SCORE 100 PER ✓	
TOTAL	Of Lower Section	➡	
TOTAL	Of Upper Section	➡	
GRAND TOTAL		➡	

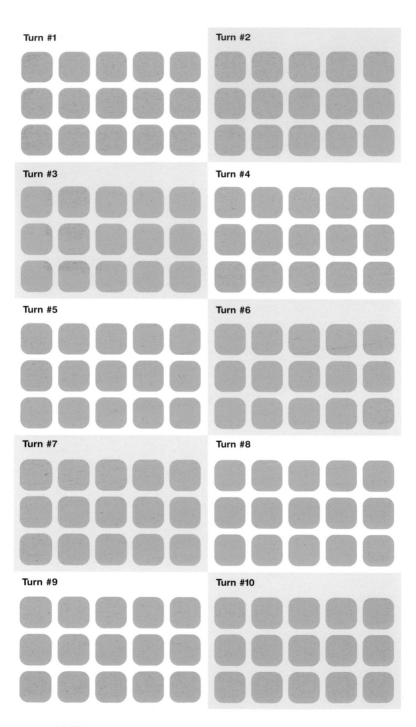

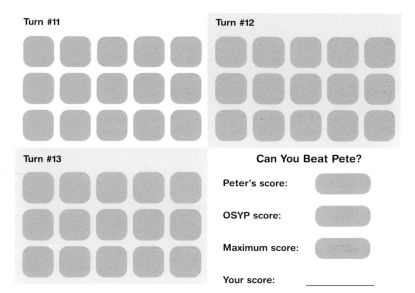

Turn #11

Turn #12

Turn #13

Can You Beat Pete?

Peter's score:

OSYP score:

Maximum score:

Your score: _____

Scratch & Play

UPPER SECTION		HOW TO SCORE	SCORE
Aces	⚀ = 1	Count and Add Only Aces	
Twos	⚁ = 2	Count and Add Only Twos	
Threes	⚂ = 3	Count and Add Only Threes	
Fours	⚃ = 4	Count and Add Only Fours	
Fives	⚄ = 5	Count and Add Only Fives	
Sixes	⚅ = 6	Count and Add Only Sixes	
TOTAL SCORE		⟶	
BONUS	If total score is 63 or over	SCORE 35	
TOTAL	Of Upper Section	⟶	
LOWER SECTION			
3 of a Kind		Add Total of All Dice	
4 of a Kind		Add Total of All Dice	
Full House		SCORE 25	
Sm. Straight	Sequence of 4	SCORE 30	
Lg. Straight	Sequence of 5	SCORE 40	
YAHTZEE	5 of a kind	SCORE 50	
Chance		Add Total of All 5 Dice	
YAHTZEE BONUS		✓ FOR EACH BONUS	
		SCORE 100 PER ✓	
TOTAL	Of Lower Section	⟶	
TOTAL	Of Upper Section	⟶	
GRAND TOTAL		⟶	

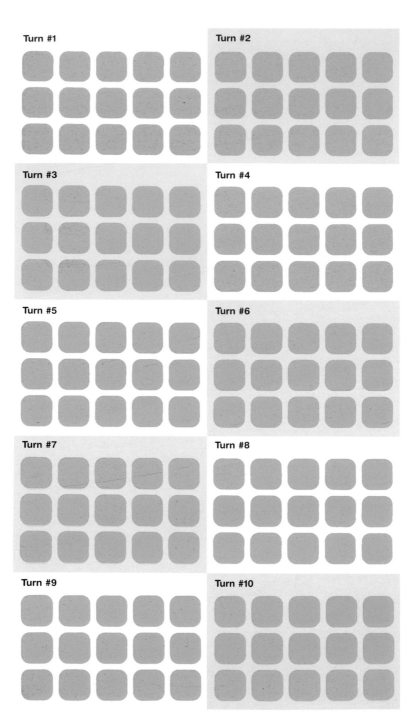

Turn #11

Turn #12

Turn #13

Can You Beat Pete?

Peter's score:

OSYP score:

Maximum score:

Your score: _____

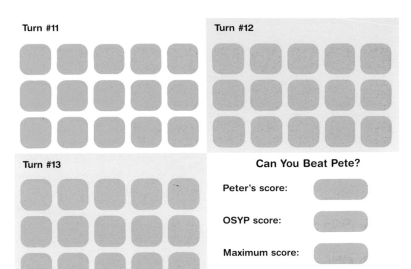

Yahtzee Scratch & Play

UPPER SECTION		HOW TO SCORE	SCORE
Aces	⚀ = 1	Count and Add Only Aces	
Twos	⚁ = 2	Count and Add Only Twos	
Threes	⚂ = 3	Count and Add Only Threes	
Fours	⚃ = 4	Count and Add Only Fours	
Fives	⚄ = 5	Count and Add Only Fives	
Sixes	⚅ = 6	Count and Add Only Sixes	
TOTAL SCORE		⟶	
BONUS	If total score is 63 or over	SCORE 35	
TOTAL	Of Upper Section	⟶	
LOWER SECTION			
3 of a Kind		Add Total of All Dice	
4 of a Kind		Add Total of All Dice	
Full House		SCORE 25	
Sm. Straight	Sequence of 4	SCORE 30	
Lg. Straight	Sequence of 5	SCORE 40	
YAHTZEE	5 of a kind	SCORE 50	
Chance		Add Total of All 5 Dice	
YAHTZEE BONUS		✓ FOR EACH BONUS	
		SCORE 100 PER ✓	
TOTAL	Of Lower Section	⟶	
TOTAL	Of Upper Section	⟶	
GRAND TOTAL		⟶	

Turn #1

Turn #2

Turn #3

Turn #4

Turn #5

Turn #6

Turn #7

Turn #8

Turn #9

Turn #10

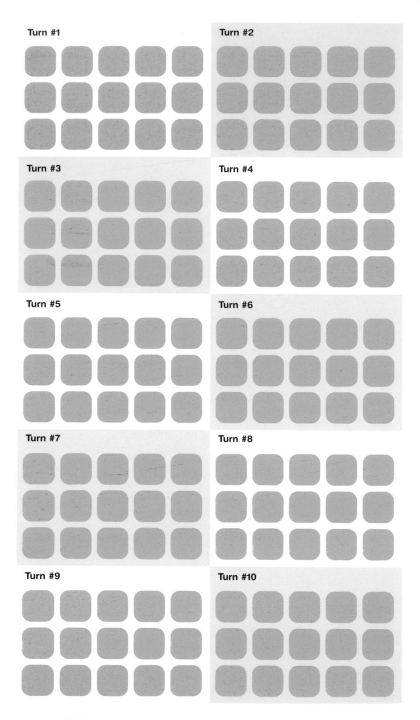

Turn #11

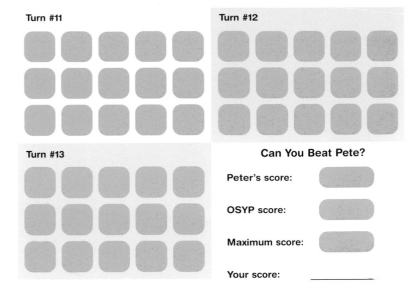

Turn #12

Turn #13

Can You Beat Pete?

Peter's score:

OSYP score:

Maximum score:

Your score: _____

Yahtzee Scratch & Play

UPPER SECTION		HOW TO SCORE	SCORE
Aces	⚀ = 1	Count and Add Only Aces	
Twos	⚁ = 2	Count and Add Only Twos	
Threes	⚂ = 3	Count and Add Only Threes	
Fours	⚃ = 4	Count and Add Only Fours	
Fives	⚄ = 5	Count and Add Only Fives	
Sixes	⚅ - 6	Count and Add Only Sixes	
TOTAL SCORE		➡	
BONUS	If total score is 63 or over	SCORE 35	
TOTAL	Of Upper Section	➡	
LOWER SECTION			
3 of a Kind		Add Total of All Dice	
4 of a Kind		Add Total of All Dice	
Full House		SCORE 25	
Sm. Straight	Sequence of 4	SCORE 30	
Lg. Straight	Sequence of 5	SCORE 40	
YAHTZEE	5 of a kind	SCORE 50	
Chance		Add Total of All 5 Dice	
YAHTZEE BONUS		✓ FOR EACH BONUS	
		SCORE 100 PER ✓	
TOTAL	Of Lower Section	➡	
TOTAL	Of Upper Section	➡	
GRAND TOTAL		➡	

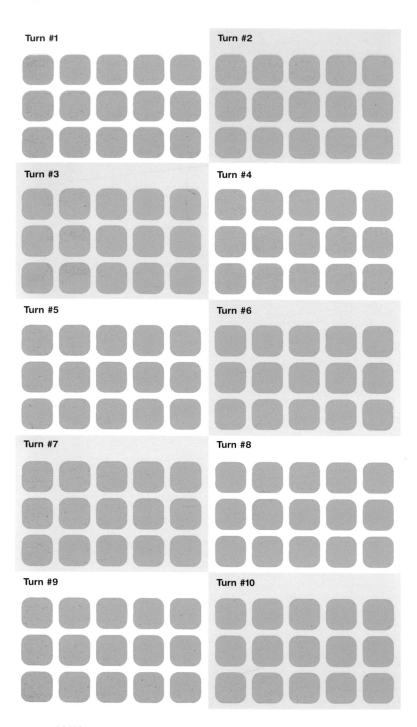

Turn #11

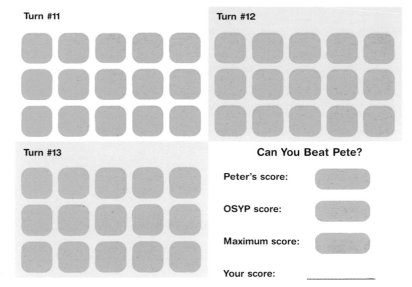

Turn #12

Turn #13

Can You Beat Pete?

Peter's score:

OSYP score:

Maximum score:

Your score: _____

Yahtzee Scratch & Play

UPPER SECTION		HOW TO SCORE	SCORE
Aces	⚀ = 1	Count and Add Only Aces	
Twos	⚁ = 2	Count and Add Only Twos	
Threes	⚂ = 3	Count and Add Only Threes	
Fours	⚃ = 4	Count and Add Only Fours	
Fives	⚄ = 5	Count and Add Only Fives	
Sixes	⚅ = 6	Count and Add Only Sixes	
TOTAL SCORE		⟶	
BONUS	If total score is 63 or over	SCORE 35	
TOTAL	Of Upper Section	⟶	
LOWER SECTION			
3 of a Kind		Add Total of All Dice	
4 of a Kind		Add Total of All Dice	
Full House		SCORE 25	
Sm. Straight	Sequence of 4	SCORE 30	
Lg. Straight	Sequence of 5	SCORE 40	
YAHTZEE	5 of a kind	SCORE 50	
Chance		Add Total of All 5 Dice	
YAHTZEE BONUS		✓ FOR EACH BONUS	
		SCORE 100 PER ✓	
TOTAL	Of Lower Section	⟶	
TOTAL	Of Upper Section	⟶	
GRAND TOTAL		⟶	

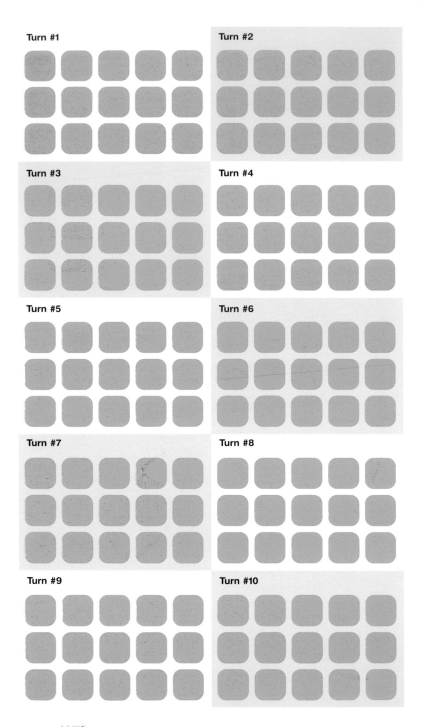

Turn #1

Turn #2

Turn #3

Turn #4

Turn #5

Turn #6

Turn #7

Turn #8

Turn #9

Turn #10

Turn #11

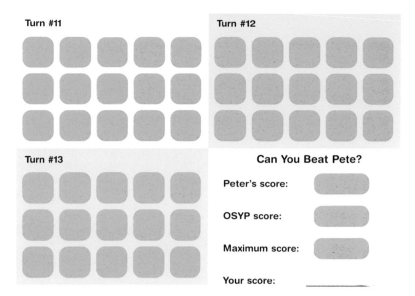

Turn #12

Turn #13

Can You Beat Pete?

Peter's score:

OSYP score:

Maximum score:

Your score: _____

Yahtzee Scratch & Play

UPPER SECTION		HOW TO SCORE	SCORE
Aces	⚀ = 1	Count and Add Only Aces	
Twos	⚁ = 2	Count and Add Only Twos	
Threes	⚂ = 3	Count and Add Only Threes	
Fours	⚃ = 4	Count and Add Only Fours	
Fives	⚄ = 5	Count and Add Only Fives	
Sixes	⚅ = 6	Count and Add Only Sixes	
TOTAL SCORE		⟶	
BONUS	If total score is 63 or over	SCORE 35	
TOTAL	Of Upper Section	⟶	
LOWER SECTION			
3 of a Kind		Add Total of All Dice	
4 of a Kind		Add Total of All Dice	
Full House		SCORE 25	
Sm. Straight	Sequence of 4	SCORE 30	
Lg. Straight	Sequence of 5	SCORE 40	
YAHTZEE	5 of a kind	SCORE 50	
Chance		Add Total of All 5 Dice	
YAHTZEE BONUS		✓ FOR EACH BONUS	
		SCORE 100 PER ✓	
TOTAL	Of Lower Section	⟶	
TOTAL	Of Upper Section	⟶	
GRAND TOTAL		⟶	

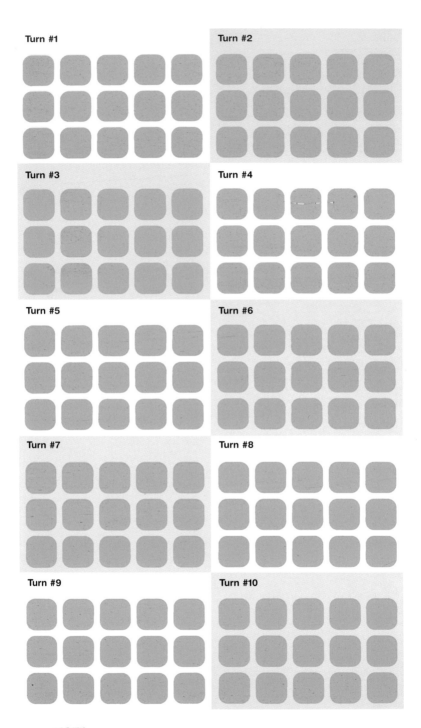

Turn #1

Turn #2

Turn #3

Turn #4

Turn #5

Turn #6

Turn #7

Turn #8

Turn #9

Turn #10

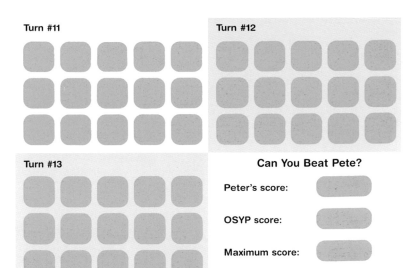

Turn #11

Turn #12

Turn #13

Can You Beat Pete?

Peter's score:

OSYP score:

Maximum score:

Your score: _____

Scratch & Play

UPPER SECTION		HOW TO SCORE	SCORE
Aces	· = 1	Count and Add Only Aces	
Twos	: = 2	Count and Add Only Twos	
Threes	∴ = 3	Count and Add Only Threes	
Fours	:: = 4	Count and Add Only Fours	
Fives	∷ = 5	Count and Add Only Fives	
Sixes	∷∷ = 6	Count and Add Only Sixes	
TOTAL SCORE		⟶	
BONUS	If total score is 63 or over	SCORE 35	
TOTAL	Of Upper Section	⟶	
LOWER SECTION			
3 of a Kind		Add Total of All Dice	
4 of a Kind		Add Total of All Dice	
Full House		SCORE 25	
Sm. Straight	Sequence of 4	SCORE 30	
Lg. Straight	Sequence of 5	SCORE 40	
YAHTZEE	5 of a kind	SCORE 50	
Chance		Add Total of All 5 Dice	
YAHTZEE BONUS		✓ FOR EACH BONUS	
		SCORE 100 PER ✓	
TOTAL	Of Lower Section	⟶	
TOTAL	Of Upper Section	⟶	
GRAND TOTAL		⟶	

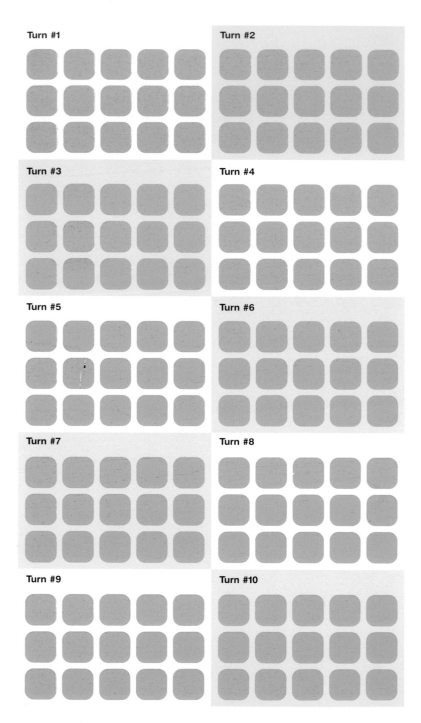

Turn #1

Turn #2

Turn #3

Turn #4

Turn #5

Turn #6

Turn #7

Turn #8

Turn #9

Turn #10

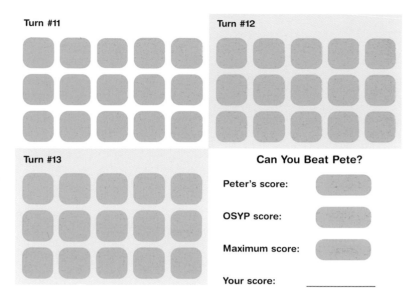

Turn #11

Turn #12

Turn #13

Can You Beat Pete?

Peter's score:

OSYP score:

Maximum score:

Your score: _____

Yahtzee Scratch & Play

UPPER SECTION		HOW TO SCORE	SCORE
Aces	$\boxdot$ = 1	Count and Add Only Aces	
Twos	$\boxdot$ = 2	Count and Add Only Twos	
Threes	$\boxdot$ = 3	Count and Add Only Threes	
Fours	$\boxdot$ = 4	Count and Add Only Fours	
Fives	$\boxdot$ = 5	Count and Add Only Fives	
Sixes	$\boxdot$ = 6	Count and Add Only Sixes	
TOTAL SCORE		$\longrightarrow$	
BONUS	If total score is 63 or over	SCORE 35	
TOTAL	Of Upper Section	$\longrightarrow$	
LOWER SECTION			
3 of a Kind		Add Total of All Dice	
4 of a Kind		Add Total of All Dice	
Full House		SCORE 25	
Sm. Straight	Sequence of 4	SCORE 30	
Lg. Straight	Sequence of 5	SCORE 40	
YAHTZEE	5 of a kind	SCORE 50	
Chance		Add Total of All 5 Dice	
YAHTZEE BONUS		✓ FOR EACH BONUS	
		SCORE 100 PER ✓	
TOTAL	Of Lower Section	$\longrightarrow$	
TOTAL	Of Upper Section	$\longrightarrow$	
GRAND TOTAL		$\longrightarrow$	

Turn #1

Turn #2

Turn #3

Turn #4

Turn #5

Turn #6

Turn #7

Turn #8

Turn #9

Turn #10

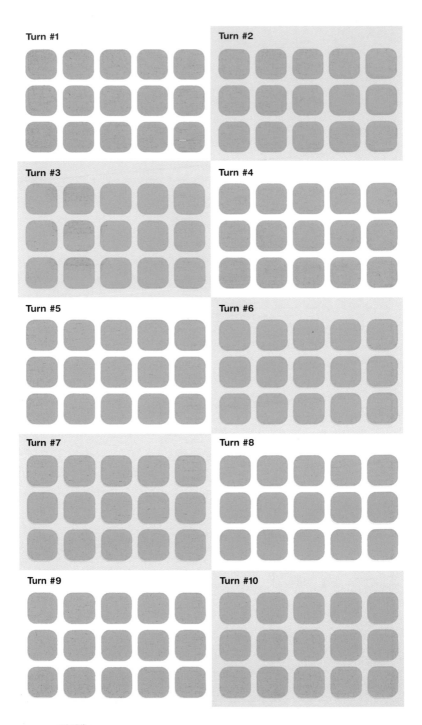

Turn #11

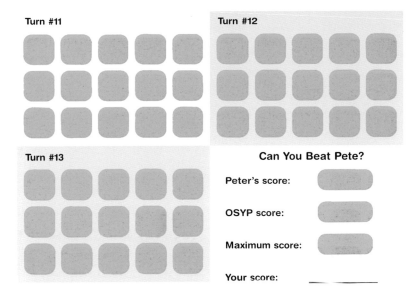

Turn #12

Turn #13

Can You Beat Pete?

Peter's score:

OSYP score:

Maximum score:

Your score:

Yahtzee Scratch & Play

UPPER SECTION		HOW TO SCORE	SCORE
Aces	• = 1	Count and Add Only Aces	
Twos	•• = 2	Count and Add Only Twos	
Threes	••• = 3	Count and Add Only Threes	
Fours	•••• = 4	Count and Add Only Fours	
Fives	••••• = 5	Count and Add Only Fives	
Sixes	•••••• = 6	Count and Add Only Sixes	
TOTAL SCORE		⟶	
BONUS	If Total Score is 63 or over	SCORE 35	
TOTAL	Of Upper Section	⟶	
LOWER SECTION			
3 of a Kind		Add Total of All Dice	
4 of a Kind		Add Total of All Dice	
Full House		SCORE 25	
Sm. Straight	Sequence of 4	SCORE 30	
Lg. Straight	Sequence of 5	SCORE 40	
YAHTZEE	5 of a kind	SCORE 50	
Chance		Add Total of All 5 Dice	
YAHTZEE BONUS		✓ FOR EACH BONUS	
		SCORE 100 PER ✓	
TOTAL	Of Lower Section	⟶	
TOTAL	Of Upper Section	⟶	
GRAND TOTAL		⟶	

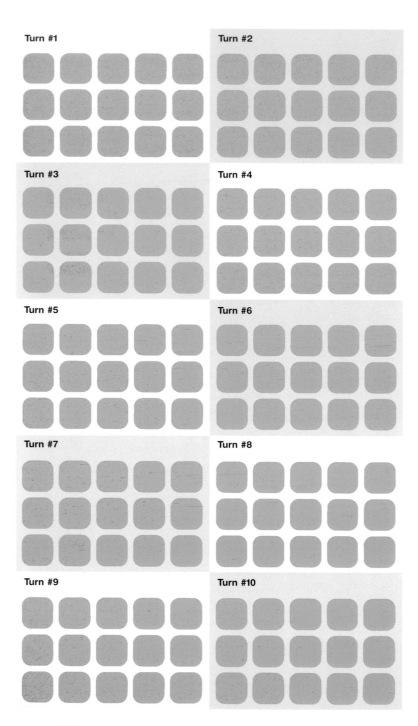

Turn #1

Turn #2

Turn #3

Turn #4

Turn #5

Turn #6

Turn #7

Turn #8

Turn #9

Turn #10

Turn #11

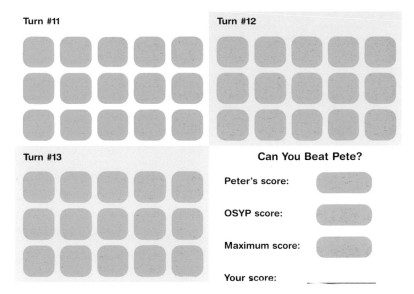

Turn #12

Turn #13

Can You Beat Pete?

Peter's score:

OSYP score:

Maximum score:

Your score:

Scratch & Play

UPPER SECTION		HOW TO SCORE	SCORE
Aces	· = 1	Count and Add Only Aces	
Twos	= 2	Count and Add Only Twos	
Threes	= 3	Count and Add Only Threes	
Fours	= 4	Count and Add Only Fours	
Fives	= 5	Count and Add Only Fives	
Sixes	= 6	Count and Add Only Sixes	
TOTAL SCORE		⟶	
BONUS	If total score is 63 or over	SCORE 35	
TOTAL	Of Upper Section	⟶	
LOWER SECTION			
3 of a Kind		Add Total of All Dice	
4 of a Kind		Add Total of All Dice	
Full House		SCORE 25	
Sm. Straight	Sequence of 4	SCORE 30	
Lg. Straight	Sequence of 5	SCORE 40	
YAHTZEE	5 of a kind	SCORE 50	
Chance		Add Total of All 5 Dice	
YAHTZEE BONUS		✓ FOR EACH BONUS	
		SCORE 100 PER ✓	
TOTAL	Of Lower Section	⟶	
TOTAL	Of Upper Section	⟶	
GRAND TOTAL		⟶	

Turn #1

Turn #2

Turn #3

Turn #4

Turn #5

Turn #6

Turn #7

Turn #8

Turn #9

Turn #10

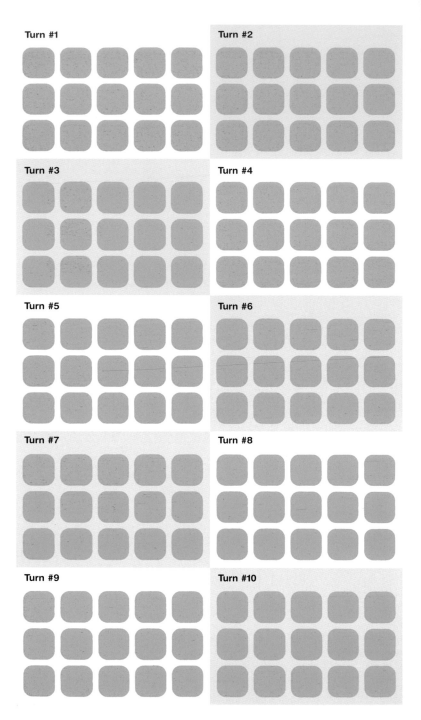

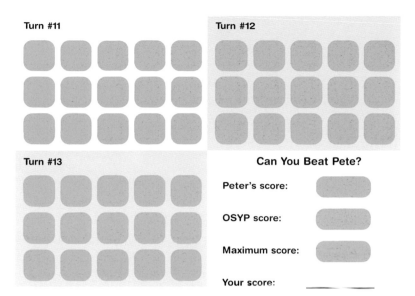

Turn #11

Turn #12

Turn #13

Can You Beat Pete?

Peter's score:

OSYP score:

Maximum score:

Your score:

Yahtzee Scratch & Play

UPPER SECTION		HOW TO SCORE	SCORE
Aces	⊡ = 1	Count and Add Only Aces	
Twos	⊡ = 2	Count and Add Only Twos	
Threes	⊡ = 3	Count and Add Only Threes	
Fours	⊡ = 4	Count and Add Only Fours	
Fives	⊡ = 5	Count and Add Only Fives	
Sixes	⊞ = 6	Count and Add Only Sixes	
TOTAL SCORE		➤	
BONUS	If total score is 63 or over	SCORE 35	
TOTAL	Of Upper Section	➤	
LOWER SECTION			
3 of a Kind		Add Total of All Dice	
4 of a Kind		Add Total of All Dice	
Full House		SCORE 25	
Sm. Straight	Sequence of 4	SCORE 30	
Lg. Straight	Sequence of 5	SCORE 40	
YAHTZEE	5 of a kind	SCORE 50	
Chance		Add Total of All 5 Dice	
YAHTZEE BONUS		✓ FOR EACH BONUS	
		SCORE 100 PER ✓	
TOTAL	Of Lower Section	➤	
TOTAL	Of Upper Section	➤	
GRAND TOTAL		➤	

Turn #1

Turn #2

Turn #3

Turn #4

Turn #5

Turn #6

Turn #7

Turn #8

Turn #9

Turn #10

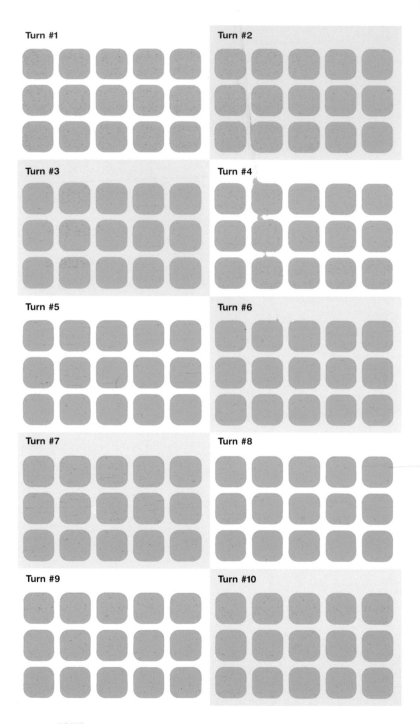

Turn #11

Turn #12

Turn #13

Can You Beat Pete?

Peter's score:

OSYP score:

Maximum score:

Your score: _____

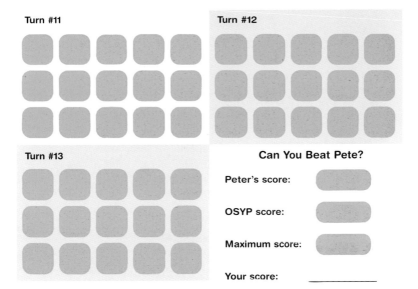

Scratch & Play

UPPER SECTION		HOW TO SCORE	SCORE
Aces	⋅ = 1	Count and Add Only Aces	
Twos	⋅⋅ = 2	Count and Add Only Twos	
Threes	⋅⋅⋅ = 3	Count and Add Only Threes	
Fours	⋅⋅⋅⋅ = 4	Count and Add Only Fours	
Fives	⋅⋅⋅⋅⋅ = 5	Count and Add Only Fives	
Sixes	⋅⋅⋅⋅⋅⋅ = 6	Count and Add Only Sixes	
TOTAL SCORE		⟶	
BONUS	If total score is 63 or over	SCORE 35	
TOTAL	Of Upper Section	⟶	
LOWER SECTION			
3 of a Kind		Add Total of All Dice	
4 of a Kind		Add Total of All Dice	
Full House		SCORE 25	
Sm. Straight	Sequence of 4	SCORE 30	
Lg. Straight	Sequence of 5	SCORE 40	
YAHTZEE	5 of a kind	SCORE 50	
Chance		Add Total of All 5 Dice	
YAHTZEE BONUS		✓ FOR EACH BONUS	
		SCORE 100 PER ✓	
TOTAL	Of Lower Section	⟶	
TOTAL	Of Upper Section	⟶	
GRAND TOTAL		⟶	

Turn #1

Turn #2

Turn #3

Turn #4

Turn #5

Turn #6

Turn #7

Turn #8

Turn #9

Turn #10

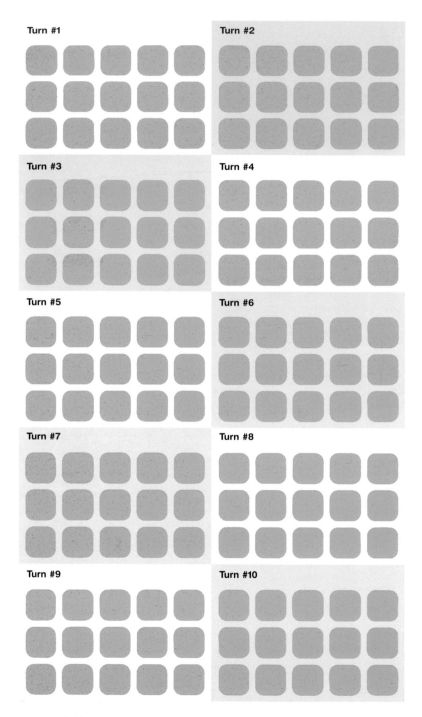

Turn #11

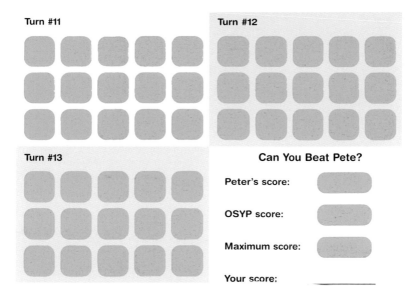

Turn #12

Turn #13

Can You Beat Pete?

Peter's score:

OSYP score:

Maximum score:

Your score:

Yahtzee Scratch & Play

UPPER SECTION		HOW TO SCORE	SCORE
Aces	⊡ = 1	Count and Add Only Aces	
Twos	⊡ = 2	Count and Add Only Twos	
Threes	⊡ = 3	Count and Add Only Threes	
Fours	⊡ = 4	Count and Add Only Fours	
Fives	⊡ = 5	Count and Add Only Fives	
Sixes	⊡ = 6	Count and Add Only Sixes	
TOTAL SCORE		⟶	
BONUS	If total score is 63 or over	SCORE 35	
TOTAL	Of Upper Section	⟶	
LOWER SECTION			
3 of a Kind		Add Total of All Dice	
4 of a Kind		Add Total of All Dice	
Full House		SCORE 25	
Sm. Straight	Sequence of 4	SCORE 30	
Lg. Straight	Sequence of 5	SCORE 40	
YAHTZEE	5 of a kind	SCORE 50	
Chance		Add Total of All 5 Dice	
YAHTZEE BONUS		✓ FOR EACH BONUS	
		SCORE 100 PER ✓	
TOTAL	Of Lower Section	⟶	
TOTAL	Of Upper Section	⟶	
GRAND TOTAL		⟶	

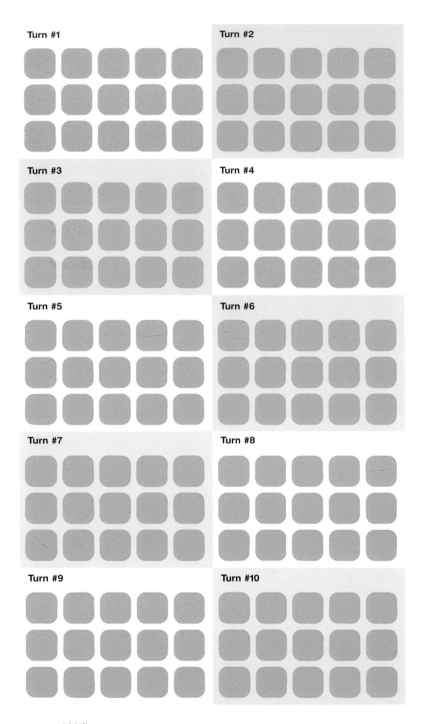

Turn #1

Turn #2

Turn #3

Turn #4

Turn #5

Turn #6

Turn #7

Turn #8

Turn #9

Turn #10

Turn #11

Turn #12

Turn #13

Can You Beat Pete?

Peter's score:

OSYP score:

Maximum score:

Your score: _____

Ya͟htzee Scratch & Play

UPPER SECTION		HOW TO SCORE	SCORE
Aces	$\cdot$ = 1	Count and Add Only Aces	
Twos	$\vdots$ = 2	Count and Add Only Twos	
Threes	$\therefore$ = 3	Count and Add Only Threes	
Fours	$\square$ = 4	Count and Add Only Fours	
Fives	$\square$ = 5	Count and Add Only Fives	
Sixes	$\square$ = 6	Count and Add Only Sixes	
TOTAL SCORE		———————➤	
BONUS	If total score is 63 or over	SCORE 35	
TOTAL	Of Upper Section	———————➤	
LOWER SECTION			
3 of a Kind		Add Total of All Dice	
4 of a Kind		Add Total of All Dice	
Full House		SCORE 25	
Sm. Straight	Sequence of 4	SCORE 30	
Lg. Straight	Sequence of 5	SCORE 40	
YAHTZEE	5 of a kind	SCORE 50	
Chance		Add Total of All 5 Dice	
YAHTZEE BONUS		✓ FOR EACH BONUS	
		SCORE 100 PER ✓	
TOTAL	Of Lower Section	———————➤	
TOTAL	Of Upper Section	———————➤	
GRAND TOTAL		———————➤	

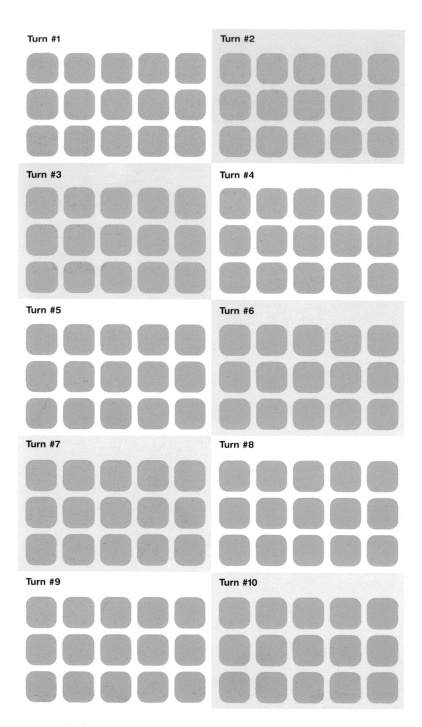

Turn #1

Turn #2

Turn #3

Turn #4

Turn #5

Turn #6

Turn #7

Turn #8

Turn #9

Turn #10

Turn #11

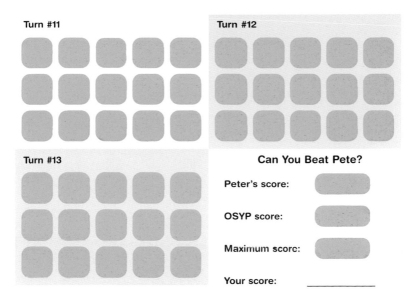

Turn #12

Turn #13

Can You Beat Pete?

Peter's score:

OSYP score:

Maximum score:

Your score: _____

Yahtzee Scratch & Play

UPPER SECTION		HOW TO SCORE	SCORE
Aces	· = 1	Count and Add Only Aces	
Twos	·· = 2	Count and Add Only Twos	
Threes	·· = 3	Count and Add Only Threes	
Fours	:: = 4	Count and Add Only Fours	
Fives	:·: = 5	Count and Add Only Fives	
Sixes	::: = 6	Count and Add Only Sixes	
TOTAL SCORE		⟶	
BONUS	If total score is 63 or over	SCORE 35	
TOTAL	Of Upper Section	⟶	
LOWER SECTION			
3 of a Kind		Add Total of All Dice	
4 of a Kind		Add Total of All Dice	
Full House		SCORE 25	
Sm. Straight	Sequence of 4	SCORE 30	
Lg. Straight	Sequence of 5	SCORE 40	
YAHTZEE	5 of a kind	SCORE 50	
Chance		Add Total of All 5 Dice	
YAHTZEE BONUS		✓ FOR EACH BONUS	
		SCORE 100 PER ✓	
TOTAL	Of Lower Section	⟶	
TOTAL	Of Upper Section	⟶	
GRAND TOTAL		⟶	

Turn #1

Turn #2

Turn #3

Turn #4

Turn #5

Turn #6

Turn #7

Turn #8

Turn #9

Turn #10

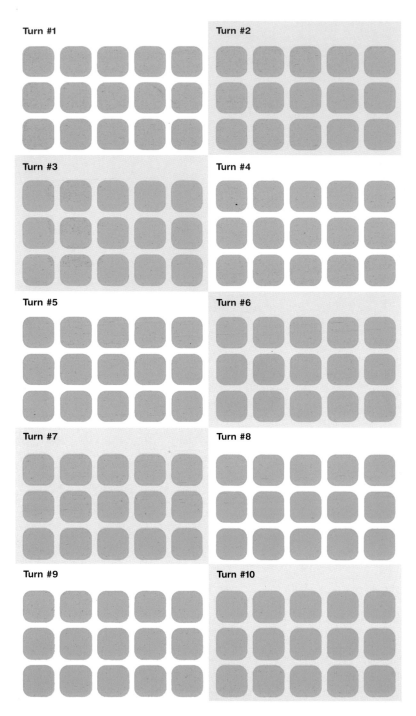

Turn #11

Turn #12

Turn #13

Can You Beat Pete?

Peter's score:

OSYP score:

Maximum score:

Your score: _____

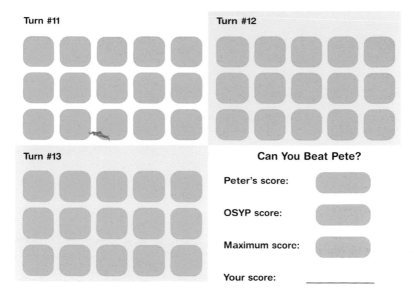

Scratch & Play

UPPER SECTION		HOW TO SCORE	SCORE
Aces	⚀ = 1	Count and Add Only Aces	
Twos	⚁ = 2	Count and Add Only Twos	
Threes	⚂ = 3	Count and Add Only Threes	
Fours	⚃ = 4	Count and Add Only Fours	
Fives	⚄ = 5	Count and Add Only Fives	
Sixes	⚅ = 6	Count and Add Only Sixes	
TOTAL SCORE		⟶	
BONUS	If total score is 63 or over	SCORE 35	
TOTAL	Of Upper Section	⟶	
LOWER SECTION			
3 of a Kind		Add Total of All Dice	
4 of a Kind		Add Total of All Dice	
Full House		SCORE 25	
Sm. Straight	Sequence of 4	SCORE 30	
Lg. Straight	Sequence of 5	SCORE 40	
YAHTZEE	5 of a kind	SCORE 50	
Chance		Add Total of All 5 Dice	
YAHTZEE BONUS		✓ FOR EACH BONUS	
		SCORE 100 PER ✓	
TOTAL	Of Lower Section	⟶	
TOTAL	Of Upper Section	⟶	
GRAND TOTAL		⟶	

About the Author

PETER GORDON, a lifelong YAHTZEE fan, keeps an Electronic Hand-Held YAHTZEE game in his car, and he prefers to be the passenger so that his game isn't limited to red lights. Not counting YAHTZEE bonuses, his highest score is 343 points, and that included taking a 0 in Aces. In another game, he scored over 700 points by getting a YAHTZEE five times in the 13 turns.

Gordon and his wife live on Long Island with his-and-her YAHTZEE games, along with their two young daughters and one old bulldog. When he's not playing YAHTZEE, Gordon spends his time editing crosswords for *The New York Sun* and daydreaming about someday breaking the 800-point barrier.